The Gloves Are Off

Maggie Kirkpatrick

THE GLOVES ARE OFF

The inside story
– from *Prisoner* to *Wicked*

NH
NEW HOLLAND

CONTENTS

Acknowledgements   6

Foreword   The Girl Next Door   7

One   Birth And Consequences   11

Two   Steel City   17

Three   Sydneysiding, New Zealandizing, Sydneysiding   33

Four   Finding Bohemia   50

Five   Livin' In The Seventies   58

Six   Prisoner Of The Eighties   72

Seven   The Year I Would Rather Forget   88

Eight   Through A Glass, Hazily   102

Nine   The Theatre Still Calls   114

Ten   Travels Through The Country   133

Eleven   Rest And Restoration   145

Twelve   Life Becomes Wicked   157

Thirteen   Tumbledown   171

Fourteen   Trial And Confabulation   182

Fifteen   The Truth Shall Set You Free (Maybe)   198

ACKNOWLEDGEMENTS

Some thirty years ago I was given an elaborate blank page book by the incomparable publicist Eileen O'Shea who, during my time in *Prisoner*, taught me all I needed to know about publicity, interviews and the media. The book has lain in a cupboard all these years, but I have finally heeded Eileen's inscription, 'O.K. Maggie, now start writing.'

So, thank you, Miss O'Shea.

My thanks, in no particular order, go to:

Xavier Waterkeyn for encouragement and support. Stephen Moriarty for setting it up and getting me into this. To Ian Bradley for giving me Joan Ferguson. To Bernadette Hayes and John Frost of the Gordon Frost Organisation for Madam Morrible – seven years of security and support along the way. To John Misto for Shoehorn Sonata. To the late Enid Rowthorne for the rounded vowels. To Craig Bennett and Craig Murchie for love and patience, and for the title. To my dear David Mitchell for unerring friendship and a great foreword.

To Wendy Becher, Peta Webb, Geoff Satchell, Robbie Mynott, Jo-Ann Richardson, Lyn Lovett and Gail Thomas who, along with many others, stood by me through the smooth and the rough.

To Judy Nunn who urged me to take on the challenge of this book. To Robert Cope for years of support and encouragement and to Mike Walsh for friendship and putting me on the West End stage.

Finally, to my family.

The unconditional love of Caitlin, Daniel and Megan is what has defined me and kept me going.

There is one thing I have always wanted to say ...

Thanks to everyone I have ever worked with for making me look so good.

THE GIRL NEXT DOOR

You'd never describe Maggie Kirkpatrick as 'the girl next door', but, to me, she was literally the girl next door.

It was the mid-seventies and I lived in Edgecliff Road, Woollahra, in an apartment building which had two basement flats. One was my friend David Penfold and I, and the other was Maggie, her husband Kirk and their tiny daughter Caitlin (already in bowler-hat, tap dancing on her parent's coffee-table!).

We shared the courtyard between our apartment – very suitable for parties. In fact, a friend of ours used to put up electric radiators in the trees and dub the soirées, 'tropical garden parties'! We didn't care as long as the flagons were plentiful, and the courtyard was filled with theatrical friends and lots of loud show music. Raucous showtunes often lingered into the night. As the night gave way to morning, Maggie would fling open her window and scream out to Penfold and me, 'For God's sake. It's three o'clock in the morning. Turn the music *up*!'

I was working on the daily *Mike Walsh Show* as a segment producer and our job was to go and find likely guests to appear on the show. There wasn't the industry of talk-show personalities in those days so to search them out one would have to go to parties, meet weird and wonderful folk and invite them to come on the show to talk about their lives. I remember meeting people who we billed as 'stripper turned poetess' or, 'legless ballroom dancers', or the elusive, 'laughing lesbian'.

Maggie was booked as 'the loud shoe saleslady'. (She was of course a very well-known actress but to the *Mike Walsh* audience she was a shop assistant who had some very funny and outrageous stories of shoe shop secrets!)

Maggie and Mike hit it off immediately – they nicknamed each other's tippling alter-egos 'Syd' and 'Pearl'. Whenever we needed someone to be fun and funny we would give Maggie a call and she would ring her employer and say that her bunions were playing up and she could be found on the *Mike Walsh Show* that day at noon!

Mike eventually cast her as one of the leads in his production of *Anything Goes*, playing one of her 'grande dame' characters. For someone so down to earth, it's funny how Maggie keeps playing society matrons in musicals like *Irene* and *Anything Goes*.

Of course, our next-door neighbour was a fine actress but had yet to make it to the big time. This seemed to loom with the imminent production of the musical *Chicago* which Richard Wherrett was directing for the Sydney Theatre Company, starring Geraldine Turner and Nancye Hayes.

Maggie thought that she would be perfect for the part of Matron Mama Morton, the very fierce and butch warden at The Cook County Jail. Mama was in charge of the 'merry murderesses', Velma Kelly and Roxy Hart. Maggie learned the song, 'When You're Good to Mama', and would rehearse it every day and every night in front of Penfold and I. We would give her notes and make sure she was ready for the audition. Well, on the day of the audition she went in did the song perfectly, and the director said, 'Sorry, Maggie. You play socialites. No one is going believe you as a fierce, butch, prison guard!' So, Maggie didn't get the part but a year or so later she morphed into *Prisoner*'s Joan Ferguson – The Freak – and proved Mr Wherrett's predictions very, very wrong!

David Penfold and I had built up quite a reputation producing drag shows at the club Capriccios on Oxford Street in the days of 'arson and amyl nitrate'. The thing that set our shows apart was that we created full mini-musicals and hired top actors to voice the characters in the shows.

The very first one we did was *Which Witch is Which?*, loosely based on *The Wizard of Oz*. We had Jeanne Little voice the character of Dorothy, whom we called 'Mabel' because there was a show called *Mack and Mabel* and we wanted to use the song, 'Look What Happened to Mabel' as the finale, so suddenly it was Mabel who went over the rainbow and not Dorothy. No one in the audience seemed to care!

Toni Lamond voiced Rosie Glow, 'The squeaky-clean, Good Witch' and Maggie Kirkpatrick was cast as Karen, 'The Wicked Witch of the Western Suburbs'. At one point in the show, when Mabel has been captured by the Wicked Witch, Maggie had to snap at the flying monkeys, 'Shut up, you ignorant baboons!'. To which the Monkeys (voiced by Tony Sheldon and me), shot back, 'We're not baboons! We're gibbons!'. Maggie answered, 'Okay, Pamela. Take Mabel somewhere where nobody ever goes. Take her to the ladies' toilet!'. These jokes might seem impenetrable nowadays but were hilarious to an audience in 1974 who knew Pamela Gibbons was a famous actress – one of Maggie's co-stars in the musical *Irene* – and who appreciated the fact that the ladies' toilet was the most deserted place in the whole of the gay club!

Well for Maggie, this gig was a 'set and forget'. It was the drag queens who had to come in every night to mime her voice. That was until the next show, *Cinderella* which had already been recorded prior to rehearsals. Geraldine Turner had already recorded one of the ugly sisters' voices with classic lines like, 'Is that Hortense?', 'No. She looks quite calm to me!'. But how Maggie ended up on stage every night in a drag show is one of the marvellous stories in this volume.

Maggie has an easy writing style and tells her story with charm, honesty and great good humour. She invests the highs and lows of her life with equal sincerity and insight. This came as no surprise to me as I had worked as co-writer on Maggie's first biographical outing, *The Screw is Loose*, a cabaret which played at Woolloomooloo's legendary pub venue, The Tilbury.

On stage and screen and now, in print, Maggie is a true original. She's a dear and treasured friend. Of course, she can be a daunting dame at times and, as 'The Freak' has managed to inject naked fear in the hapless viewers simply by donning those menacing leather gloves.

However, don't be daunted as you turn the page. I guarantee you're going to relax and enjoy the experience, now that *The Gloves Are Off!*

David Mitchell
May 2019

David Mitchell

David most recently co-wrote *Doris: So Much More Than the Girl Next Door* with the show's star, Melinda Schneider. *Doris* has played successful seasons in Brisbane, Melbourne, Adelaide and at The Sydney Opera House.

With Melvyn Morrow, David co-wrote *Shout! The Legend of the Wild One*, starring David Campbell. in 2000, when it broke box-office records around Australia.

David was also co-writer of the successful musical production, *Dusty*, which grossed twenty-five million dollars and won four Helpmann Awards in 2006, and Melbourne's Green Room Award for Best New Australian Production.

David has written for Barbra Streisand, Bob Hope, Michael Parkinson, Barry Humphries, Clive James, Ronnie Corbett, Lorna Luft, and the late Danny la Rue.

A prolific freelance television producer, David's shows include, *The Mike Walsh Show, Parkinson, Saturday Night Clive, The Dame Edna Experience, Barry Humphries' Flashbacks* and *This is Your Life*.

His Royal Bicentennial Concert in 1988 which starred Olivia Newton-John, Peter Allen and Kylie Minogue, amongst many others, was described by showbiz bible, *Variety*, as, 'pure, unremitting, unalloyed, entertainment!'.

He is currently devising a one-man show with Cameron Daddo.

CHAPTER ONE

BIRTH AND CONSEQUENCES

I have a fairly comprehensive history of my father's family, a little of my maternal grandfather's history and until very recently virtually nothing of my maternal grandmother.

Information has come my way regarding 'Clan Campbell' which was my grandmother's maiden name. Family secrets were uncovered, and I found it fascinating.

My grandmother was born in 1873 in Bungaree, on or around the goldfields of Ballarat. She was christened Christina Catherine. Her parents were Peter and Caroline Campbell. Peter had been born in the parish of Dunoon-Kilmun, Argyllshire, Scotland in 1835 and migrated to Australia between 1853 -1860. He married Catherine Bennett in 1873. Catherine was the seventh child of Isaac and Ann Bennett. Isaac Bennett, my great, great grandfather had been transported to the colonies in 1835, arriving on the *Recovery* February 26, 1836. He had been sentenced in the Essex Quarter Sessions to seven years for embezzlement.

I recall asking my mother, years ago, about the family history. She intimated that a member of her family had done a little research and horror, horror, a convict was found! Back then it was considered a terrible blot on family names. Nowadays, it seems to be a badge worn with pride. I for one am certainly delighted.

Another little piece of unknown family history is the fact that my grandmother in 1896 gave birth to Alfred Thomas Campbell who was raised as a member of Peter and Caroline Campbell's family. An illegitimate child absorbed into the family was not unknown. I believe that my mother has gone to her grave not knowing that she had another brother. Alfred is listed as the eighth child of Peter and Catherine.

I am intrigued by a little snippet of research that shows in almost all cases, either side of my family history, births of offspring almost without exception were within a very few months of a marriage taking place. It seems that my daughter Caitlin and I, making our own choices, would both avoid the 'shotgun wedding'.

And so, we come to January 1941.

War was raging in Europe. The population of Australia was 7,109,898. RG Menzies was Prime Minister, FDR was inaugurated for the third time as President of the USA. Classic films such as *The Maltese Falcon* were released, Billie Holiday was singing 'God Bless the Child'; 'Chattanooga Choo Choo' was a best seller on Top of The Pops. The destruction of Pearl Harbour brought the U.S.A into the war later in the year.

Ginger Rogers won best actress Oscar for *Kitty Foyle*.

James Stewart won best actor Oscar for *Philadelphia Story*.

Rebecca, directed by Alfred Hitchcock, won best film Oscar.

Average cost of a house was $4,075.

Average annual wage was $1,750.

Churchill launched his 'V' for Victory' campaign across Europe.

The classic Orson Welles film, *Citizen Kane* premiered.

Placido Domingo, Paul Anka and Neil Diamond were born.

The evacuation of allied soldiers from Dunkirk in northern France took place with the loss of many lives, in spite of the valiant efforts of coastal Britons and their volunteering of small boats.

In Albury, NSW, Crissie Downs (nee Davies) gave birth to a baby girl, Margaret Ann Downs. I was born on Wednesday January 29 around 7.00 a.m. at Meramie Private Hospital.

My father, Alfred James Downs, was serving in North Africa with the 2nd/32nd AIF soon to be at Tobruk.

Crissie was a country girl born in Tasmania and raised in Grenfell,

NSW. She was the youngest of five children born to Christina Campbell and William Davies. From working in a haberdashery store in Grenfell, she was transferred to Rutherglen, Victoria, to manage a branch of that store.

It was here she met my father. He was a handsome, devil-may-care man-about-town. He worked in the Great Southern mine, served in the Militia and played Australian rules football for Rutherglen Football Club. His mother, Annie, ran a local pub, The Royal Standard and he was the eldest of ten children – eight girls and two boys.

The Downs family in North East Victoria were descended from Enoch Downs (1831-1883) who, as an adventurous 21-year-old, had arrived in Australia with the hope of finding his fortune on the goldfields of Victoria. He had come from the Potteries region of Staffordshire in Northwest England. It was expected that he, like all in his family before him, would become a potter. The Downs family history in that region dates back to 1651 with Guilielmus Downs. We always assumed that he too was from the North West of England.

It was into this family that I arrived. The first grandchild. Crissie and I took up residence in the pub.

My mother told me that we were housed in great-grandfather Young's room, situated beyond the back bar of this single-storey pub. Apparently it was not uncommon for the room to be used as an escape route when the local constable raided after-hours drinkers. These escapades might well have been my first, but certainly not last, encounters with drunks.

Family myth has it that my dummy was often dipped in gin to pacify me. Oh dear, was that the start of it all? My lifelong 'affiliation' with pubs and alcohol.

So it was that my life began surrounded by loving adults. Eight aunts – Noel (Noakie), Nancy, Lola, Wilma, Joan, Mavis, Ailsa, Gwenda and, a teenage uncle, Stanley (Sonny), my doting grandmother Anne Downs (nee Young), and my beautiful mother, Crissie. I take it I was rather spoiled by all this attention and even at around the age of two or three I was known to stand on the bar of the pub and sing wartime songs such as 'Brown Slouch Hat' and 'Bell Bottom Trousers', obviously loving the attention lavished on me by all. My mother always called me 'Margaret', but my grandmother and aunts persisted with the diminutive, Peggy — a throwback to Irish forebears somewhere along the line, no doubt.

But back to 1941 — August 10 to be exact.

On a beach in North Africa, my father was killed.

Having been in the trenches for weeks on end, beach parties were organised so that the men could wash and rid themselves of lice and whatever other ghastly things affected them. On this day, my father, Lieutenant Alfred James Downs, was the Officer of the Day and took a small group of his men to the sea shore that they might give themselves some respite from the trenches. After washing away the filth, they sat down on the beach to dry off and were attacked. My father died instantly. As I understand it, he and his men were picked off by an Italian sniper.

Two other members of the group died the next day. I don't know any more than that.

Back in Australia, my then 24-year-old mother was facing a life without Jim. So, there she was, in a country town with a new baby and a large but very new family of in-laws. What could have been going through her mind? As related to me by my mother, it appears that on the day she received the news of my father's death she had experienced a feeling of unease throughout the day. To relieve this, she put me in my pram and took off to visit friends. Curiously, wherever she went, no one was at home. This added to her feeling of foreboding. On returning home, a visit from the local Church of England minister brought her the news.

I was never really able to ascertain just what her immediate reaction was.

One thing I am sure of is that her strongest will was about to be put to the test as she faced raising a child on her own in the days when single mothers did it hard.

After a couple of years, John Anderson came into her life. He was a soldier just back from the Middle East and he was about to be sent on to the New Guinea campaign. He was stationed at Puckapunyal, 196 km from Rutherglen. Social activities for the entertainment of the troops stationed there were big events in the surrounding small towns. Rutherglen was no exception and the outgoing Downs family led by my gregarious gran Annie were in the thick of the socialising. Picnics by the Murray River, dances, and all manner of social activities. I'm sure all this was carried out with great fun and frivolity in spite of the wartime anxieties that must have been felt.

At one of these outings Crissie met John. I have no idea of the attraction between them. Crissie was a very attractive brunette who loved to dance. John, from all accounts, was quite shy. Originally from Newcastle, NSW, and previously married but now divorced, he was the eldest of three children. He had a sister Joan and a brother Bob, who at the time was a prisoner of war, taken by the Germans during the Crete campaign in Greece 1941, after the disastrous Greek campaign.

The late Lt-General John Coates summed up the campaign thusly:

'Yet, as in almost every Allied campaign in the early part of the war, the worst mistakes of the politicians and strategists were moderated by the bravery, fighting qualities and sheer dogged determination of the troops. Greece was no exception.'

The attraction between Crissie and John continued to blossom and, after a period of time, it was decided that my mother and I would move north to Newcastle, to be there when the war was over. I must have been about three at the time. Our departure was met with hostility by my aunts but apparently my grandmother simply said to my mother, 'Don't ever do anything to hurt Peggy' and gave us her blessing.

I like to think that my mother's whirlwind romance with my father had been the stuff that wartime romances are made of. The sense of urgency, of uncertainty, I'm sure added to heightened passions.

Perhaps I have simply been the victim of too many Hollywood movies.

I asked my mother, some forty years later, if Jim was the love of her life. Her answer brought tears to both of us as she agreed that he was indeed her Great Love. She also wondered if it would have lasted had he returned. It seems that his outlook on life was not as orderly as my mother's. My father, as already mentioned, had somewhat of a fun-loving, devil-may-care attitude – a prankster and one of the boys. Maybe that's where some of my somewhat incautious attitudes come from. Most unlike my mother's circumspect ways.

I have it on good authority from a friend of his whom I had the pleasure of meeting in Rutherglen. Colin Diffy was a local farmer, friend and senior officer who knew my father very well. He assured me that Jim was one of the finest men he had known. I am so pleased that I met this delightful gentleman before he passed away a little time later. He put my mind to rest regarding the character of the man I never knew.

So, it was off to Newcastle where the next twenty years would shape what was to become of my life.

CHAPTER TWO

STEEL CITY

Newcastle, the second city of NSW, is a beautiful coastal city – a former convict colony with some of the most spectacular beaches in Australia. It was also Australia's largest steel producing and shipping city. Coal from the Hunter Valley was shipped through the port of Newcastle all over the world. During the war it had been a target for the Japanese submarines that had been attacking the coastline and it had been shelled in June of 1942.

Newcastle was indeed a Steel City and the great mining company, BHP, was king. The wealth of the area was dependent on that great industry. In the retail businesses of the city it was most apparent. Fortnightly pay packets meant that every two weeks was mini boom time. Strikes in the coalfields or the factories affected everyone. Life was good, if perhaps a little parochial, but I, like many former Novocastrians, praise and defend it to this day.

Mum and I stayed with John's parents, Verlie, a gentle creative soul, and Tom, a sadistic brute who played the double bass in the city orchestra. He loathed me on sight and wouldn't allow me to eat at the table when he was at home. It was with Bulla the dog I took my meals when old Tom was around.

Eventually, Mum fostered me out to a middle-aged family with a teenage daughter. Because of Tom? I'm not sure. Perhaps it was simply that as she worked she wanted an orderly life for me in a friendly environment.

At least then she knew I was in caring hands when she was at work. The Audsley's filled that bill. Dick Audsley was too old to go into war service, so he was a bus driver – an essential service. My mother was then working as a 'clippie' or conductress, one of the many necessary jobs to be filled by women during wartime.

My time with the Audsleys wasn't too traumatic, although they did tease me about the dark and all that 'boogie man' stuff until a pathological fear of the dark was instilled in me and didn't go away until I was about sixteen.

I also began kindergarten in my time at Merewether, although my memory of that school is pretty hazy. It didn't leave much of an impression. Maybe that's where my ambivalence toward school began.

But one thing does stand out: when my mother came to see me on her days off, she asked what my teacher was like.

'Oh, Mummy, she's lovely. She's just like you only she has blonde hair.' A fairly accurate description to my young eyes. Imagine my Mother's mirth when she discovered that the teacher was about sixty years old and had WHITE hair!

My passion for peanut butter was discovered round about this time. Food was still rationed and something like peanut butter was considered a luxury. Coupons were required, even though the war was over. Dick Audsley made sure that Mum had some of his ration coupons in order to keep me stocked with P.B.

The love for that spread continues to this day and in fact my school lunches were no problem for my mother – just peanut butter, year in and year out. Except sometimes on a Monday when the fresh bread hadn't come. Then, it was really treat time, a MEAT PIE washed down with a new soda pop called COCA COLA. …. WOW!

At this time, Mum and I became involved with Legacy. This wonderful organisation had been set up after WW1 to assist widows and children of fallen comrades by servicemen who had returned from conflicts.

We were under the guidance of Colonel John Mather, himself a decorated war hero. His role was that of mentor and adviser. I believe that it was his influence and guarantee that enabled my mother to put a deposit on a house – a rare thing for a single mother in those days. It enabled me to return to my mother, and with the help of a retired couple as boarders and baby sitters we moved into the house in the lakeside suburb of Belmont possibly late '46 or early '47.

Every Friday night I would go into the city to Legacy House and take part in the activities designed for us kids. We had physical culture classes (as they were called back then) – a cross between callisthenics and dance movement, and all of it extremely good for posture and well-being. There were also craft hobby classes and the thing I loved most – elocution and drama. These classes were taken by a wonderful woman named Enid Rowthorne. She had been engaged before the war but her fiancée in the Air Force never returned. She was to become a huge influence in my life in a few years' time.

The war had ended, and John Anderson was home from New Guinea. My mother's relationship with him seemed to have cooled. I don't really know about the 'cooling off period' with John Anderson. Perhaps it was simply a lover's tiff. As a child I was not privy to the reasons why. 'Children should be seen and not heard.'

It wasn't until 1947 that they were finally married. So, now we were a family. John was gentle, kind and funny, and treated me with the love and care of a real father. Our happy little family was completed in 1948 with the arrival of my baby brother, Adrian. I must say that I was embarrassed by that name – there weren't any 'Adrians' in my school, so I told everyone his name was John. I suspect there was a small case of 'nose out of joint' on my part because now had to share my life with another child after having been the golden girl for seven years.

But any childish resentment I might have had at this 'intrusion' into my domain was quickly dispelled. Adrian grew into a *most* adorable child, possibly a *little* spoilt but no more so than I had been. He was the apple of my mother's eye. Apparently my mother used to warm the toilet seat for her little boy!!! I don't actually remember this, but my sister in law assures me it is so. That's taking motherly love to a whole new level!

In his adolescence he was a good student and a loving son. I left home when he was twelve, so I wasn't around for much of his teenage years, but like I had before him, I think he enjoyed the Newcastle way of life. In adulthood he has become my 'big' brother. Although seven years my junior he has a been a constant source of support and comfort when I needed it. His no-nonsense approach to life is matched by his loyalty to friends and his love of family. He and his wife Cheryl have raised two wonderful people, Bill and Sarah who, in turn, have become parents to Indigo, Solomon and Harris. Grandchildren have given Adrian and Cheryl a precious gift in their retirement and they are deeply involved in the lives of their family.

I think Adrian inherited our mother's ability to manage money. He is a whiz in the budgeting department. I like to think that he developed his good taste in clothes due to the fact that when 'big sister' was working he received the trendy clothes of the day. Desert boots and Ivy-League shirts were *de rigueur* for a time.

But back in the late 1940s Australia still had post-war rationing and some of the little memories have stayed with me: going to the corner shop with the ration book and buying a small piece of butter, or a small amount of broken biscuits, all put in brown paper bags. It was around about this time I used a public phone for the first time. We certainly didn't have one in the home. I can remember being quite terrified as I put one penny in the slot and then had to actually speak to someone. Boy, did that fear disappear! The telephone seems to have been surgically attached to me ever since. Especially when the 'pub phone' became my obsession, as many can attest to.

As a small child I was loud, inquisitive and opinionated. Some might say that nothing much has changed. My outspokenness was evident in such moments as when I was seated on a tram opposite a pregnant woman. My loud voice (even then) boomed out, 'Mummy! Why is that lady so fat?'

Travelling with my mother on a train to Albury for some 500 kms, we were seated opposite a man with no teeth. As if that wasn't fascinating enough to my four-year-old eyes, I was transfixed by what he did when we stopped for a cup of tea and a biscuit (as was the practice in those days). He dunked his biscuit in the cup of tea. I had never seen this before. Naturally, I had to copy him and, along with my childhood love of peanut butter, I have been dunking ever since.

My birthdays came around at the height of summer during school holidays and we were invariably away camping. My mother always endeavoured to get a watermelon. Although nowadays they are available all year round, back then they were at their peak in January and it was a wonderful treat. My mother used to hollow out the melon and fill it with delicious fruit salad. An ice cream birthday cake completed this yummy summer treat.

As a pre-teen I was constantly poring over movie magazines and oohing and aahing over Marlon Brando, Tony Curtis, Rock Hudson, Doris Day et al. I would hopelessly try to recreate the song and dance routines of Debbie Reynolds and Carleton Carpenter like 1951's *Aba Daba Honeymoon*. I was an avid movie goer long before I became an usherette at the Civic Theatre. My mother had always taken me to see those great movies of the 40s and 50s, classics that I find hard to better to this day. We frequently visited her brother Lew and his wife Bonnie on their dairy farm in Grenfell, in western NSW. While there we would keep up our practice of movie going. In those days, movies opened in Australia long after the USA and country towns saw movies long after they had been seen in Sydney.

So it was not unknown for me to loudly pre-empt the film's plot and tell all around me that 'Bambi's mother is going to die' (one of the iconic tragic scenes of the cinema) or to jump in and loudly sing 'Run Little Raindrop Run' before poor Betty Grable could get a word out.

By 1950, we had moved to another suburb and to a larger house set on quite a large block. At this time, I suspect that funds were low with only one wage coming in because for two years or more, my mother grew all our vegetables, tended fruit trees, raised chickens and made all our clothes including pyjamas and winter coats. The bread was delivered by a baker in a horse drawn cart and the 'dunny' man came each week to empty the outside lavatory. Although this was the time of the polio epidemic and outings to crowded places were a risk, we had fun at home. We had a radiogram and lots of records that Mum and John would dance to: Glenn Miller, Perry Como,

Bing Crosby. I lived in a fantasy world of Debbie Reynolds, Doris Day and MGM musicals, giving my versions of these to anyone who would listen or watch me cavorting around as if I were Ginger Rogers. It was a happy time of my childhood in that house.

I spent my last years of primary schooling in Cardiff. I recall those last two years to have been most stimulating. English and history fascinated me and would continue to do so throughout my life.

History in general. Ancient and modern. The history of the British monarchy fascinates me, and that's coming from an avowed republican. As for literature, I have devoured books from the moment I could read. When out for family Sunday drives, I drove my family mad by reading every sign we passed. As the years went by, sitting in the back seat of the family car, there was never a peep out of me as my head was firmly locked in my latest reading matter. Fiction, non-fiction, poetry and Hollywood fan magazines – they all captivated me.

A stimulating and committed teacher was all it took and happily, Cardiff Primary School gave me just that.

Culturally, also, my senses were being awakened by the presence of children from Europe. These were the post-war migrants, survivors of those horrendous years. There was a migrant camp nearby and I was fascinated by the Polish, Latvian and Italian kids who came to the school, and their presence made me hungry for more knowledge from outside my little world.

In my last year at that school our end of term play was to be Dickens's *A Christmas Carol*. I *desperately* wanted to play Scrooge, but that honour went to Ken Longworth and I had to settle with playing the three ghosts. Ironically, Ken went on to become a journalist and theatre critic. In later years he was most flattering in his reviews of my work.

And so to high school …

Once again, my almost total indifference in the day-to-day workings of being educated raised its head. Except, of course, for English and history classes and music. My love of language, history and poetry came alive under the guidance of three remarkable, gifted and charismatic teachers.

Teacher's names are lost in the mists of time. I do, however, recall a Miss Guthrie, Eula, I believe was her name. She made English and history come alive for me. I was, however a noisy, rather disruptive influence in the class room. Class clown, probably. Somehow Miss Guthrie treated my interjections with some humour. When bandying words with me she would sometimes hurl a piece of chalk at me with the words, 'Lousy pun, Anderson, lousy pun!'

Then there was a Mrs. Wilson, petite, peaches and cream complexion, and a gift for making teenage girls appreciate music other than the emerging rock and roll. She opened my eyes and ears to classical music and to Gilbert and Sullivan.

Once again, guidance was all I needed to whet my appetite for learning, although that appetite was really only interested in those particular subjects. Actually, almost all of my school reports stated that 'Margaret excels in subjects which interest her'. Looking back now, I see that the curriculum of the day was really very stodgy. Outside my frustration with some of the curriculum, school wasn't without its fun. Parrying witticisms with a fabulous English teacher who didn't seem to object to my being a bit of a class clown, and a production of Gilbert and Sullivan's *Iolanthe*. Imagine a lumpy fourteen-year-old 'tripping hither, tripping thither, nobody knows why or whither' in a green cheese cloth fairy costume.

I particularly loathed maths and never in my years of schooling did I ever get a pass mark. My high school maths teacher was a Mrs Griffiths and she looked and behaved as if she should have been retired years before. She was a tyrant and a bully, who only had time for students who understood her wretched maths and made no attempt to improve the knowledge of the students who didn't.

Although, to be truthful, I really wasn't interested. Probably a pity because I have been appalling with money all my life. Many years later I was making my professional debut with the John Alden Shakespeare Company. While waiting for a bus one evening after a performance I spotted Miss Guthrie leaving the theatre. Sadly, I was too shy, even at the age of twenty, to approach her. I wonder if she was proud of noisy Margaret Anderson who delivered lousy puns all those years ago?

However, much to the disappointment of Mrs. Wilson and Miss Guthrie I left school a month before my fifteenth birthday.

In the past I have often asked myself, with some regret, why?

Regret, because for many years I thought that my lack of 'education' limited my options. Acting is a risky business – an understatement if ever there was one. In the early years I had nothing really to fall back on. What if I hadn't 'made it'? And yet, I also believe that having nothing to fall back on spurred me to make a success of acting.

And also, for many years, I'll admit that I occasionally I felt that I'd missed out on something, *academically*.

Yet now, looking back, whatever regrets I may have had about leaving school have been dispelled by my experiences of life. What I missed out on academically, I feel I have made up for by my innate inquisitiveness and the strongest desire to be a bit of a know-all. I have found *life's* education has stood me in reasonable stead, as well as the desire to keep on discovering and learning. So, I don't dwell too much on those lost school days, they weren't all that crash hot anyway. I don't think I have turned out too badly in the intellect stakes.

*   *   *

I started work immediately in a dress shop.

The junior.

Dusting, packing, making cups of tea and getting the other girls' lunches. Such a stimulating job for a fertile imagination. Not!

I was pretty much a loner. I had discovered classical music and my head was never out of a book except for perhaps when I was at the movies or day dreaming. So, when I started my first job – for five pounds a week – I joined the World Record club and each month a classical recording would arrive in the post. It was the beginning of educating myself to the beauty of classical music. I simply ordered the album of the month and piece by piece developed my appreciation. At the time I was particularly taken with the drama of Beethoven and Tchaikovsky, but as the years have gone by the works of Mozart, Elgar and Vivaldi are among my favourites.

I had also renewed my interest in performing and took lessons from the Miss Rowthorne who had so captured my imagination at Legacy. It was under her tuition that I performed verse speaking and character pieces at local Eisteddfod – competitions of performance, music and literature. With some modesty I will say that I won just about every competition that I entered.

I was completely absorbed in this world of Shakespeare, Shaw, Dickens et al and not even *remotely* interested in the social life of the average teenager of the day. Social life of teens in Newcastle at that time consisted mainly of flirting at the beach, dances at the Palais, and smooching in the back row at the movies. Not for me.

It would be remiss of me not to mention a little more about the beach culture of those days. Life was simple and safe and from an early age we travelled without parents. Newcastle Beach, Newcastle Baths and the Bogey Hole were our destinations – a day spent in the sun and the water covered in an oil and vinegar mixture to promote a tan. Little did we realise that this nonsense was cooking us as we burnt and then peeled and then browned. We revelled in it. Leaving the beach as the sun was fading and the shadow had covered the beach we would head for the fish and chip shop and then indulge in a little shy flirting with some gangly youth at the bus stop. The Bogey Hole was saved for when we were older. It is a heritage-listed sea bath which was hewn out of the rock by convicts on the orders of Commandant Morisset in 1820 for his own personal use. It is a wonderful, crystal-clear pool with waves occasionally breaking over. Many years later, when I was pregnant, we used to go swimming at night in this pool in the hope that I could hasten an already overdue baby's arrival.

But that was in the future. In this now I had become a somewhat over-imaginative and over-romantic teenager.

Radio plays captured me. To visualise a drama simply through the magic of words was heaven to me. Little did I know that in a few years I would be working with some of my radio heroes and heroines like Lyndall Barbour, Ron Haddrick, Neva Carr-Glynn and Tom Farley – to name a few.

I did go to a concert once at the cavernous Newcastle Stadium. It was the era of Lee Gordon in Sydney bringing popular American artists to Australia for the first time. That night I saw Bill Haley and the Comets – hot on the heels of the release of their soon-to-become-anthemic, 'Rock Around the Clock' – The Platters and Lavern Baker. In 1957 I went along to see Little Richard, Gene Vincent and Eddie Cochran.

Curiously at this time, despite all my cultural pursuits, I was determined to be a nurse.

I'm not sure just what caused me to have that youthful desire to be a nurse. I suppose I always had somewhat of a nurturing bent in me. As a child I was forever bringing home stray dogs and cats. Sometimes they weren't even strays and they had to be returned to their owners! I suppose my penchant for waifs and strays continued into my adult life. Maybe that's why I later involved myself with deadbeats – some high hopes of changing their ways and showing them a better life. Who knows? Maybe I should have had a religious calling and become a missionary? Anyway, my search for causes often led to decisions that seemed perfectly normal, *at the time* – like joining the Communist Party, handing over a cheque for $1000 dollars in a pub one night so that a teenage refuge might stay open a little longer, or contributing a ridiculous amount of money at a showbusiness event in London so that a young person could have a much-needed wheelchair. Perhaps my life would have been a whole lot simpler if I had become a nurse, settled down, married a doctor and stayed in Newcastle for the rest of my life.

Then again, I would have missed out on a *lot* of fun.

Anyway, the desire to be a nurse soon changed.

After leaving the dress shop, I became an usherette at the fabulous Civic Theatre. Now, I was *really* able to indulge my love of movies. In those days there were two feature films plus newsreels three times a day. Cinemascope came along. *The Robe* starring Richard Burton was the first one ever, and the first one I ever saw. How we lapped up these big screen extravaganzas! People queued for hours to wait for the next session. Saturday nights they dressed up and we usherettes showed them to their numbered seats. We had to memorise the entire seating plan of the theatre. Cinema-going back then was a very social affair.

For me, watching a movie some twenty or thirty times was sheer bliss.

During my time as an usherette at Newcastle's Civic Theatre, I worked with women considerably older than I was. Well, when you are sixteen, anyone over twenty-five seems old. My co-workers, to me, all seemed so sophisticated and I would look on in awe as they dolled themselves up after work to go on a date. They were elegant and stylish in my eyes, their makeup and hair immaculate. They would be off to meet their dates and whirl away in smart European cars for a night out and I would catch the bus home to suburban Waratah. I was intrigued one night when one of the particularly glamourous women, in fact a Marilyn Monroe look-alike, was preparing to meet her boyfriend. After she had repaired her makeup, fluffed up her hair, she proceeded to spray perfume between her legs. I found this incredulous and stared in amazement. She never did tell me why, but it certainly dawned on me some years later.

One night after work I was invited to supper by one of these sophisticates. With permission from my mother (yes, that's right), I accompanied her to the Great Northern Hotel, which in those days was the epitome of glamour and sophistication. It was a grand Art Deco hotel frequented by the wealthy people of Newcastle and for those days, that description is not an oxymoron.

So, there I was, sixteen years old out with the grownups. I was treated to an elegant supper of dainty sandwiches such as chicken and, yes, cucumber and, wonder of wonders, a glass of Pimm's No1 ....

'WOW!' I thought, '*This* is living!'

To top the evening off, the string quartet played excerpts from the new hit musical *My Fair Lady*. Neither the stage show nor the album had been released in Australia, so I suppose it was an early example of pirating.

Home I went on the late bus with the Lerner and Lowe music in my ears.

Under the influence of the magic of movies and rubbing shoulders with glamour, my plans to become a nurse were fading fast.

So, once again, I decided to spread my wings and move on. This time to a newly-opened branch of the prestigious department store David Jones. There, in their very smart shoe department, I was trained to be a shoe fitter and sales girl, selling everything from bedroom slippers to high-end *Ferragamo* and *I. Miller* fashion shoes.

My long-delayed social life began when the city opened its first coffee lounge, *The Brazil*, which became a haunt for all sorts of people who were regarded with suspicion by the locals. Heavens above! These people sat around drinking coffee, talking, playing chess or reading poetry! What hell is this to have come to our respectable town? Were they beatniks? After all, the girls wore black stockings, had long hair and wore no makeup. The boys had beards and wore duffle coats and suede desert boots. They sported dark glasses day and night and sometimes they went to the pub, drank pints of beer and sang folk songs!

The good folk of Newcastle were outraged. Even the Bodgies and Widgies had been more acceptable than this lot.

Well, *I loved it!* I had found my niche. Out went the floral dresses, hooped petticoats and gloves, and in came the baggy sweaters, long hair and black stockings. In order to appease my appalled mother, this garb only came out at weekends, and then in secret before I got to the pub or the coffee shop.

Wow!

Was *I* living!

So the rebellion had begun. In the eyes of my family, I was destined for no good – to be sold into prostitution, abducted by aliens and who knew what else. There was concern about 'that back room of the coffee shop' because 'Heaven knows what goes on in there!' Well, as far as I could see, it was simply a storeroom.

The café was presided over by the vivacious Rosa and frequented by many Italians. I was fascinated by their continental ways, their charm, their language and clothes. Here was the cosmopolitan life I was looking for.

Slowly, these wonderful newcomers began to change the 'meat and three veg' world of Newcastle.

Cafés opened and began to serve real Italian food, with wine too! The foods that now seem to be the staple diet of Australians, spaghetti Bolognaise, ravioli, Parmigiana, and minestrone were finally changing our palates forever.

My love of all things Italian was blossoming. Soon other European cultures came our way as Greek and Eastern European cafés and clubs opened.

We were slowly coming out of our stifling, Anglo conformity.

In the late 50s and early 60s our favourite meeting place, along with the Brazil Coffee Lounge, was a pub called The Beach Hotel. Here the welcoming atmosphere developed into a sort of mini 'push' as influenced by the Royal George 'push' in Sydney – both pushes were a bit like 'The Algonquin Round Table', but with more beer involved.

In the back bar of this unremarkable pub gathered a motley lot of musicians, students, tradies, and retail workers such as myself, and a general collection of non-conforming Novacastrians. We drank beer by the pint, because it was cheap, and songs and laughter rang out until closing time. Folk songs, protest songs and blues were the order of the day. Guitars, bongo drums and sometimes a trumpet or clarinet joined in.

The Beach Hotel was owned by a most colourful character. Arthur Greenhalgh was a showman of the old school who, along with his partner American Ernest Jackson, formed the then renowned business of Greenhalgh and Jackson. They imported many acts to Sideshow Alley and promoted the famous Boxing Tents.

Arthur began his career in 1910 and until his death in 1972 remained one of Australia's leading sideshow entrepreneurs.

The walls of the pub were plastered with photos of some of his acts, 'Chang, The Pin-Headed Chinaman,' and Dennis O'Duffy, 'The Irish Giant.' There was also The Bearded Lady, The Three-Legged Man and The Siamese Twins – to name a few.

The outbreak of World War Two put a temporary end to show business and in 1943 he bought the hotel where he housed some of his overseas acts who were stranded for the duration. Apparently, 'The Giant' washed the windows (without a ladder), 'The Midget' tapped the barrels and 'The Fat Lady' and 'The Tattooed Lady' presided over the kitchen.

During our time as the 'young rebels' of Newcastle, many famous acts stayed in the pub. Once, a production of *Snow White and the Seven Dwarfs* came to town, and the cast of 'dwarfs' was housed at the pub. Sometimes in the saloon bar they would join in the fun, using the bar stools as their bar. I actually found them a bit scary, besides they were rather randy little fellas and my crotch was level with their eyes! It took a bit of ducking and weaving to avoid unwanted contact. My fear of 'little people' went way back to when as a toddler, I had been frightened by an African Pygmy at the Easter Show – Princess Ubangi was her name. It was a phobia that lasted until the seventies when I was in a show where one of the stage hands was a person of short stature. Over a period of time and some stimulating conversations with Ross, the said short person, I overcame my childhood fear.

Back to Arthur and the pub. Bert Anderson was the manager and made us all feel as though it was a home away from home. One of our mates was a Scottish troubadour who had a wealth of folk songs and bawdy pub songs, bordering on the obscene. He renamed the pub, The Dunkirk. The reason? 'It was the "Bloody" Beach!'

Arthur's wife, Fuschia was as exotic as her name. When she wasn't away selling tickets to their sideshows, she sat at the end of the bar not exactly holding court but just being a decorative presence. When it was time for her to go upstairs to their residence, usually when Arthur thought she'd had enough to drink, she would often slip some money into my hand and say, 'Get me a bottle of sherry will you love, and don't tell Arthur.' I would do so and sneak the bottle upstairs to her. Fuschia died in 1963 and rumour has it that she died in a ticket booth, selling tickets to the end.

Of course, all those colourful 'freaks', as they were called, no longer appear in Sideshow Alley. Political correctness, rightly so, has stopped the exploitation of not only the characters but of the gullible crowds. As PT Barnum allegedly said, "There's a sucker born every minute" and no more so than in Sideshow Alley.

I had discovered so much more of life by this time that my desire to be a nurse had completely vanished.

I now, seriously, thought about becoming an actor.

Another discovery around this time was sex. It was no big deal, no moving earth or heavenly choirs just a decision to cease being a virgin and get on with my life. A friend obliged.

Losing my virginity at the age of nineteen wasn't a romantic undertaking. It was *purely pragmatic*.

I wanted to get on with life and sex is a part of life and I was missing out! The deed was done without bells and whistles and, I have to admit, it was really rather boring. Happily, later on, it got better. The friend who obliged ridding me of the encumbrance known as a hymen served society well. I understand he enabled a couple of my female friends to also get on with their social lives.

What a community spirited man!

Jazz also played a big part in our lives back then. There were several budding musicians in our group and we frequently went to Sydney to hear the bands on offer there. Graeme Bell, The Port Jackson Jazz Band, Merv Acheson and Dick Hughes. For modern jazz we headed to the basement venue in Kings Cross, El Rocco, where we listened to Judy Bailey, Mike Nock, Bryce Rohde, Don Burrows among others.

The Royal George became our pub of choice when in Sydney. This was the home of the 'Sydney push' of artists, writers, students, libertarians – the bohemian centre of Sydney.

It was also the days of candles in Chianti bottles, sea-grass matting and Spanish bullfight posters.

The days of political protest were to come. These were the calm-before-the-storm days of hedonism, promiscuity and bucking the system.

My twentieth birthday was celebrated at the Royal George. Here I met a very attractive man. He was an arty bohemian type and whisked me away on his Vespa to his studio in Kings Cross where we sat, yes, on sea-grass matting and drank Sake and yes, I do believe there were candles in Chianti bottles ... but no Spanish posters. I felt as if I were in a Parisian garret. That man went on to live in New York and became one of the most famous sculptors of his generation, noted for his massive outdoor steel sculptures.

CHAPTER THREE

SYDNEYSIDING, NEW ZEALANDIZING, SYDNEYSIDING

I now decided that Sydney was the place for me. It was time to follow my dream of being an actor.

So, much to the dismay of my mother, I left my secure job at David Jones and set off for Kings Cross. A job was needed, so I took my shoe selling skills to a very chic store, Reynolds, in the arcade of the grand Australia Hotel. I lived in a boarding house and I had the obligatory Spanish poster and candle in the equally obligatory Chianti bottle.

My accommodation at the Kings Cross Boarding House comprised of one room and a shared bathroom and kitchen. In the kitchen we all had our own spaces for supplies and there seemed to be an honour system at play because I was never aware of any food pilfering incidents. Among the residents of this very ordinary establishment was a group of wharfies – stevedores working on the docks at nearby Woolloomooloo. They were a great bunch of down-to-earth, hard-working men. After a tough day on the wharves, they would come back and cook themselves a hearty meal and then, showered and fed, they were ready for their nightly beers. If I happened to be in the kitchen at this time they scooped me up and took me with them to the pub. They were like my own protection unit. At the nearby pub, The Rex, women weren't permitted to drink inside at the bar. We had to drink out on the footpath or in the hallway leading into the bars. A ridiculous, archaic ruling but fairly standard for the times. One evening it began to rain and so they moved inside to the bar and took me with them. We were seated at a table and an officious little man in a grey dustcoat (the picker upper of empty glasses) came to us and said, 'she can't drink in here' to which my militant companions replied, 'Either she drinks in here or this pub is on the black!' Which meant a boycott, and with it the lucrative income from the wharfies would be severely diminished. Needless to say, I stayed and enjoyed my beer until we were ready to leave.

On other occasions my 'minders' would take me to another drinking spot. Sometimes a fight broke out and they would put me up on the bar, give me their drinks to mind, get on with the fight and, when it was over, resume drinking. Yes, they did get me back down off the bar too!

Those men were a great introduction for me not only to the pub culture of Sydney but to the egalitarian spirit of honest, hard-working men. It stood me in good stead years later when I met Norman Kirkpatrick who possessed those same qualities.

It might seem crazy today, but things really were different back then, and being a woman and having access to what was seen as an all-male domain was a big deal. This entrenched sexism didn't resolve itself until the late 20th century.

For example, in the late sixties when I had become the young bride Kirkpatrick and with a young daughter, the three of us were living in Balmain. In those days the Sydney inner-city suburb of Balmain was comprised of the remains of old, working-class houses. But by then, the slow, inevitable process of gentrification had begun and continues to this day. Balmain, with its proximity to the city – especially by ferry – was a magnet for young professionals of the day. Real estate was still affordable and there was a village air about the suburb. Much of that old, working-class, rough-and-tumble atmosphere still existed – especially in the presence of the abundance of pubs. Renovating Victorian terraces and worker's cottages had become a vibrant industry. Of course, nowadays, those restored houses are in the million-dollar, if not multi-million-dollar range, and luxury cars in double-garages have replaced the old Kombi vans and modest minis of yesteryear.

We made friends with like-minded couples. Our children became friends. Dinner parties and barbecues were lively events as we all shared varying political beliefs and discussions were … *robust* to say the least. One thing that we all agreed on was our opposition to Australia's involvement in the Vietnam War and the conscription that had been introduced. Harbouring young draft resisters on the run was not unknown. Although we had separate dwellings there was an attitude to communal living and, in a simple form, we often pooled resources such as bulk-buying fruit and vegetables at the market and sharing them amongst us. While we were on our rounds baby-sitting was shared or the kids came too.

As I have said there was an abundance of pubs in the suburb and some still favoured the old rules of pub segregation. Men in the public bar and the 'little woman' in the 'snug' or parlour shelling the peas.

In these first days of rebellion, the Women's Movement was in its infancy and change was in the air. We had all read Germaine Greer's *The Female Eunuch* and although many of us were not quite the bra-burning type, we felt a change coming as we asserted ourselves a little more. A moment that has stayed with me all these years was on a New Year's Eve and Kirk and I were on our way to a party. We stopped at our local pub to purchase some supplies when lo and behold a woman with friends walked out of the public bar!

Unheard of!

That woman? It was Germaine Greer herself and she had graced the all-male domain with her presence. Well, I saw that as an omen of times to come and indeed it was. Before long, women were permitted into the public bar. Mind you, most of us stayed in the lounge bar but we had the choice and so too did our men.

With all those pubs around us we had jazz bands everywhere. Lively times were had as most of us were jazz enthusiasts and we could choose venues all over the city every weekend.

With all the socialising, infidelity was rampant and not many marriages survived. It was a period of promiscuity and hedonism but, *boy, it was fun*!

I loved my time there and I made many friendships. It was a time of great change, socially and politically; a time I remember with fondness.

Women weren't the only people who led lives restricted by the norms of the time. By the time I moved to Kings Cross the Rex Hotel had a back bar that was frequented by homosexuals. I use that word because the word 'gay' wasn't around then. Back then, 'gay' was a word that simply meant light-hearted and carefree. The late Peter Kenna once said, 'I've been a homosexual all my life and there's been nothing "gay" about it!' At this time homosexuality was illegal so such establishments were quite daring. Once, on a dare, I ventured into this all-male domain. It was really a ridiculous effort in light of today's attitudes. I piled my long hair up under a cap, donned a trench coat and swaggered up to the bar and in a butch contralto voice ordered a drink. The male bartender was dressed in basic black and the only sign of flamboyance was his string of pearls! I was served my drink and thus won the dare. How ridiculous! Today, if women were not permitted all I would need to do is slap on the makeup, overdo the clothes and the hair and say 'darling' a lot and I would pass for a drag queen. No trouble at all.

Kings Cross, in those pre-Vietnam War R&R days, was a vibrant bohemian enclave.

Eccentrics abounded. Among them was Rosaleen Norton, whose fearsome occult murals adorned the walls of the Kashmir Coffee Lounge. Rosaleen Norton's murals were the stuff nightmares are made of. They consisted of witches, warlocks, pagan rituals and orgies and of course homage to the God Pan, whom I understand she worshipped. The 'Witch of Kings Cross' was certainly a colourful character in the days of real characters and eccentrics in the wonderful bohemian world that was Kings Cross.

There was also Bobby Nugent, the acclaimed motorcycle rider as well as the cross-dressing Strong Woman and the African pygmies brought to

Australia for Sideshow Alley, who lived in a flat above Darlinghurst Road. It is rumoured that they painted the refrigerator with nail varnish using the teeny little brushes and there was the S.P. (starting price) bookie who offered me a very well-paid job to take the telephone bets (he liked my voice) but I would have to pay my own fines when the police raided.

I politely declined.

Those were the days when cross-dressing was illegal, along with homosexuality, and many a hapless drag queen was arrested and even bashed by the local police.

The heady days of the Jewel Box and Les Girls were yet to come.

Then there was 'Last Card' Louie and his strip clubs.

Last Card Louie owned the Pink Pussy Cat Strip Club and was an acquaintance during my early years in the Cross. He was charming, sophisticated and a lot of fun. I remember once sitting in a booth having coffee with Louie and we were joined by one of his star strippers. She was tall and elegant, with a mane of fabulous red hair.

During the conversation she turned to me and asked, 'Are you *square*?'

Now to me, in those days, that meant to be 'uncool' – not 'with it'. My innocent answer was, 'No, I'm not square'.

At which point she moved closer to me and this prompted Louie to pull me away and quickly say, 'Yes, you *are*!'

It seems that in her vernacular to be square was to be sexually 'straight'. That was a BIG eye-opener for the kid from Newcastle who hadn't met any lesbians, *yet*.

Years later when living in Woollahra, I noted that a very chic store in that most affluent of suburbs was owned and run by Louis and his wife.

Yes, there was crime and corruption – it is a given in New South Wales – but I revelled in this mad world.

All too soon it was time to get down to the nitty gritty of my raison d'être.

I enrolled in classes at the Independent Theatre which was run by the actress Doris Fitton – very much 'The Grande Dame'.

The curriculum was very much along the lines of an English drama school. No Stanislavsky or Method here. Speak clearly with beautifully rounded vowels, walk and sit gracefully and above all, PROJECT!

It seems that my years with Enid Rowthorn held me in good stead. I complied with all of the above.

In a very short time, dear Miss Fitton decided that I 'was too far advanced' for her class and so I was promoted to the senior class run by actor/producer John Alden, who was noted for his annual Shakespeare seasons.

Maggie Dence, Donald McDonald and David Goddard were among my classmates and all of them went on to have distinguished careers.

After one term, John Alden invited me to join his Shakespeare season.

The plays were to be *Macbeth*, in which I would play one of the three witches; *Othello*, a lady-in-waiting and *The Merchant of Venice* when I would be an assistant stage manager, tea maker, stage sweeper etc. All of this was a dream come true.

To add icing to the cake, I was working with names that I knew from my passion for radio plays. Among them were Frank Waters, Hilda Scurr, Muriel Steinbeck, Marion Johns, Max Osbiston and dear Tom Farley, who years later would play my husband in an Irish play called *Da*, which we performed with the Old Tote Theatre company.

The season played at Cremorne (the Orpheum Theatre, now a magnificently restored Art Deco theatre owned by my friend Mike Walsh), The Sydney Conservatorium and the Elizabethan Theatre at Newtown.

John Alden played Othello (rather badly as I remember and with the now totally unacceptable 'black face'). Reviews were mixed for all the plays but how could I forget one for *Macbeth* which claimed that 'Hilda Scurr played Lady Macbeth like a harassed Wahroonga (a posh Sydney suburb) hostess and only the three witches gave an inkling as to how Shakespeare should be played. My name was at last in print, if not in lights.

At the end of this season, I felt daunted by the prospect of starting out, finding an agent, looking for work, auditions etc. I needed someone to tell me just *what I should do*.

But would I have listened?

Probably.

If someone older and wiser were to offer me the sort of advice available to young actors today, things just might have turned out a bit differently.

So, I went back to Newcastle and the course of my life was to change beyond all expectations.

I soon reacquainted myself with the old crowd. Some had stayed in Newcastle, some had sought fame and fortune overseas. It was the time of the great exodus of young creative folk to Europe, seeking more fertile ground for their talents than the perceived cultural desert of Australia.

We all had plans to board those P&O liners and experience the great adventure. I never did keep that rendezvous with my friends Paul Jones and Jan Nixon. It was to have been midnight, New Year's Eve on the steps of Sacre Coeur Basilica in Paris. Such a youthful fantasy! It was to be another twenty years before I made that trip. Although they didn't wait for me, Jan Nixon and I remained friends until her death in 2018. I have remained friends with Paul to this day.

I slipped back into the life of pubs, parties and Jazz Club. Of course, I had to work, so I began training as a psychiatric nurse. I was stationed at Stockton Mental Hospital, as it was called in those days. It was no trendy clinic for pampered souls. Patients were there for life, either left at birth by parents or older people with severe dementia. There was no actual treatment as such, just a lot of sedating drugs. Even young people with Down Syndrome were placed there. It's so different to today, when people like a niece of mine, Connie Kirkpatrick, who has Down Syndrome can live a full productive life and even play in a rock band which she did with great aplomb and actually went to New York with the group, banging away on her tambourine.

Nursing practices were *appalling* by today's standards. We nurses had heavy sedating drugs such as Largactil in our pockets which we popped willy-nilly into the mouths of recalcitrant patients. Barbaric? Yes, indeed it was.

It didn't take long for me to realise that this life was not for me. Besides, the matron wasn't too thrilled with me scrambling through the nurse's home window in the wee small hours after a big night out.

I managed to obtain a job as a doctor's receptionist. This I enjoyed immensely. I seemed to satisfy my medical curiosity without having to deal with the gory bits. Besides, I felt I looked rather fetching in the white uniform. I always did love dressing up.

One night in my favourite pub, I was introduced to a very charming Irishman.

Although introduced to him as Margaret, he responded with 'Hello, Maggie. Bend down so I can kiss you.'

Funny bugger?

Yes.

Did I?

Yes.

Well, he was somewhat shorter than my 175 cm.

This was Norman Kirkpatrick, merchant seaman. He was originally from Belfast and, like his three elder brothers, had run away to sea at a very young age. He was the fourth son of Annie and John Kirkpatrick. Annie was a weaver in the mills of Belfast and John had been a riveter in the shipyards.

From all accounts, John had been somewhat of a violent drunk, so badly behaved that he was thrown out of the RUC. The RUC is the Royal Ulster Constabulary, or The B Specials, a quasi-military reserve police force, known for excessive violence during the troubles of the 20s and 30s. This, of course, could have been a flight-of-fancy on Norman's part, but then, who's to know?

Annie immigrated to Australia without John, naturally, to join her older sons who were already settled in Melbourne.

'Kirk', as he was mostly known, was the last of the family to arrive. He had stowed away on a ship out of Canada and, when in international waters, gave himself up and allegedly had a pleasant journey playing chess with the captain. Well, that's *his* story anyway.

After a brief period and two marriages in Tasmania and Melbourne, he arrived in Newcastle to work on the harbour dredges.

He was a self-educated, articulate man with a great love of history, literature, the arts and was passionate about politics. His bedside reading included Jack London and *The Communist Manifesto*. Yes, he was a communist. Not through some radical, university education but a lifetime observing the injustices of the world. Although not exactly a Svengali, his influence on me and the formulation of my social and political ideals stays with me to this day. I rather suspect that some of those attitudes were lying dormant in me and simply needed to be discovered through the passions of this amazing man.

He was thirteen years older than I and offered the sort of sophistication that I had found lacking in men of my own age.

I was hooked.

As the relationship developed, it was agreed that we would move in together. This caused huge eruptions of outrage from my mother, whose major concern was, 'What will people say?'

This was such an irony considering that a few years down the track she would live for some thirty years with a man in a state of unmarried bliss.

So, to avoid continuing drama, we were married at the Registry Office. Such a sham! Kirkpatrick was not yet divorced from his second wife, so I became a bigamist ... or was I enabling bigamy? I don't know. In either case I had become complicit in breaking the law just to appease my mother. Bigamy! Sounds *so* like a Victorian melodrama. Makes me sound like such a 'scarlet woman'!

And so began the next fifteen years of my life.

In these happy days of early marital bliss I changed careers again. A large department store – 'THE STORE' is how it was known – was a Co-operative Society (or a Co-Op as they were known, particularly in the UK) I believe it simply means that the business is owned by the customers or 'the cooperative'.

The Store had installed a broadcasting booth. In a little studio, I broadcast events and specials available to customers. I would visit all the departments, take note of goods they wanted advertised, write the copy and then broadcast it throughout the day. I also arranged and compered occasional fashion parades. It was a fun job in a most pleasant atmosphere, made all the more enjoyable by the people I encountered there, one of whom was Jenni Brickett. She worked in the advertising and promotions department and went on to become a noted fashion stylist in Melbourne. She is a dear friend to this day.

Once, during a Newcastle University Prank Day, I was taken 'hostage' by students who stormed the broadcasting booth, tied me to a chair and proceeded to make hilarious announcements over the P.A. system. The management weren't too thrilled about it, but I thought it was great fun and provided a bit of offbeat humour for the customers.

Through the left-wing movement I made contact with the Newcastle branch of New Theatre.

New Theatre was founded in 1932 in Sydney and was known as The Workers Art Club. Its slogan was 'Art is a Weapon.' New Theatre is to this day the longest continuing theatre in Australia and for eighty-five years has been at the forefront in the fight against Nazism, Apartheid, the Vietnam War and censorship.

My first play was Brendan Behan's *The Hostage* where I was able to trot out my Irish accent for the first time, playing Meg. The second was *The World of Shalom Aleichem*, playing a peasant goat seller. This was no mean feat as I was about seven or eight months pregnant at the time and was required to squat on a very low stool in order to mime milking a goat. It became hell trying to get up again.

Prior to being pregnant, one of my busiest times was being secretary of the 19th Australian Jazz Convention. Given that Newcastle had such a lively jazz scene it was only natural that our city should host such an event. The Australian Jazz Convention began in 1946 and, still going, is the longest running annual jazz event in the world. It is a week of non-stop traditional or 'trad' jazz, parties, dancing, and beer, beer, beer!

So, on with the marital bliss and the much-wanted pregnancy. It was an absolutely textbook perfect pregnancy, marred only at the end by an emergency Caesarean section. So much for my plans of an easy, non-intervention birth. Oh well, nobody's perfect.

On February 1, 1966, Caitlin Jane Kirkpatrick came into our lives. I had never considered myself to be especially maternal, but to hold such a precious little person in my arms dispelled all those doubts. The love was instant, unconditional and unwavering to this day in spite of the many obstacles that life has thrown in our way, and that I myself have thrown in our way.

Three months later, it was decided that we three would embark on The Big Adventure. It was to be a trial period in New Zealand before heading to Israel to hopefully work on a Kibbutz. What a pipe dream! This was before the Six Day War and I suspect that my romantic idea of such a thing was due to an overactive imagination on my part, and empathy for holocaust survivors and their struggle to get to the 'homeland.' It was part pioneer and part Hollywood fantasy on my part and the desire for communal living on Kirk's part. We should have simply packed up and headed for the hippie communes of the New South Wales north coast. It would have been cheaper.

When I left Australia, I did so with a heavy heart. My mother had begun experiencing the horrors of domestic violence. My sweet-natured stepfather had become a violent drunk, putting my mother's life in danger. It became apparent that he was suffering from what we now know as PTSD, but then it was labelled 'war neuroses' and this was twenty years after the war. His doctor simply gave him more and more heavy sedatives and, when combined with alcohol, this caused a terrifying change in him. My pleading with the doctor for intervention fell on deaf ears as the doctor maintained that no help could be given unless he asked for it. That was never likely to happen as he and my mother were intensely private people. So the bruises were covered, and the silence maintained.

Eventually, my mother left and virtually went into hiding until there was some resolution. She never went back.

In New Zealand, I managed to get a job first, so Kirk became the stay-at-home dad. He did a superb job in those early months with our beautiful daughter.

I found work managing the New Zealand branch of the famous June Dally Watkins Modelling and Finishing School.

Do I hear a chortle?

It was a breeze. I simply hired the best that Auckland had to offer to teach deportment, etiquette, make up and modelling. It was a fun, rewarding job and I enjoyed it immensely. However, New Zealand in 1966 was even more parochial than Newcastle and so, some months later it was decided to close the business and return to Sydney.

One of the rewards of that experience was to see some of the graduates of the school go on to grace the catwalks of Europe.

On our arrival back in Sydney, it was essential that Kirk go back to sea in order to earn money for us. Through the kindness of his best friend, Tas Bull, Caitlin and I were able to stay for a short period with a schoolteacher friend in Paddington while I began to search for somewhere to live.

The house in which we stayed was a typical terrace house of that suburb. Anne, the friend who was leasing it, said that it belonged to an artist. This meant very little to me at the time, as I settled into the task of house hunting and being a mum.

Some fifty years later, I realised that this house in Duxford Street actually belonged to the great Australian artist, Margaret Olley. Now, as I volunteer at the Tweed Regional Art Gallery and Margaret Olley Art Centre, I am surrounded by her wonderful paintings and constantly peek into the re-creation of her studio/house in which I had lived for a short time all those years ago. The reproduction of Margaret Olley's house is amazing. All the paraphernalia she surrounded herself with has been faithfully reproduced, even down to cigarette butts in ashtrays. It is a highlight of the gallery and attracts visitors from far and wide as it keeps up the legacy of this most remarkable of painters. I say 'painter' as opposed to 'artist' because Olley referred to herself as a painter and her 'house' was her studio.

We finally later settled on an apartment in Bondi with the merest glimpse of the ocean. The flats on the top floor where we lived were mainly occupied by Hungarian families and some of Caitlin's first words were in Hungarian with a touch of an Irish accent – if you can imagine that! The wonderful cooking smells that emanated from next door inspired me to put goulash, chicken paprikash, dill pickles, stuffed capsicums and cabbage rolls on our menus.

After a settling in time, I reacquainted myself with the Sydney branch of New Theatre.

What a great move this was! New Theatre was situated in a back lane of inner-city Darlinghurst, right in the middle of the red-light district. In fact, I was often accosted by a 'working girl' while waiting for a bus and told to 'get off her patch'. It was always a relief when the bus came, not only to get away from the girls, but the punters as well. I simply regarded it as a fact of life in that seedy part of Sydney. Unlike today, with all the drug-related violence, no one in their right minds would stand on street corners in certain parts of the city.

At the theatre I was warmly welcomed by Marie Armstrong and Miriam Hampson, the redoubtable secretary of the theatre committee. These two women have had a most profound effect on me, theatrically and politically. They were both assertive, independent women before the women's movement became the norm. Miriam Hampson, secretary of New Theatre for many years, was the daughter of a prominent Melbourne Jewish family who protested alongside the then Archbishop of Melbourne, Cardinal Daniel Mannix against conscription and Australia's involvement in World War One. Strange bedfellows indeed, as Miriam's parents, the Aarons, were foundation members of the Communist party. Miriam's brother Sam fought in the Spanish Civil War and her nephews were officials of the Australian Communist Party for many years. Marie is a friend to this day, albeit via email and phone, and at the time of writing Marie is 91 years old and still has the vibrant political and social chutzpah she had all those years ago.

The first play I did was a World War 2 drama, *Postmark Zero*, a series of vignettes from the German point of view in letters to and from the Russian front at the Siege of Leningrad. It was directed by Roger Milliss and it was in this production that I met John Hargreaves. John was an immensely talented actor, a schoolteacher at the time, but would go on to be one of the finest actors of his generation. We became firm friends and he remained close to me and to Caitlin until his untimely death in 1996. I miss him to this day.

Other productions I was cast in were Thornton Wilder's *Skin of our Teeth*, playing Sabina, *Disorderly Women* and two other productions that were to influence me.

America Hurrah was written by Jean-Claude van Itallie, an American playwright whose opposition to the Vietnam War produced this controversial play. It was a far cry from my previous theatre experiences, but it proved to be a challenge which I readily embraced. It was my first encounter with director John Tasker and we would go on to do another six plays together. John had been considered somewhat of an *enfant terrible* by the conservative theatre establishment. His controversial productions, particularly the plays of Patrick White, caused much twittering among the good burghers of Melbourne and Adelaide. His falling out with the Nobel Laureate White was the stuff that theatre gossip thrives on. John was stimulating, frustrating and argumentative but never boring. Over the years, he never lost that fire and I loved him for it. We locked horns many times, but our friendship never wavered. John died in 1988.

America Hurrah was the catalyst for change of the censorship laws of New South Wales. New Theatre was no stranger to government interference. In 1936, their production of Clifford Odets' *Till the Day I Die* was banned in response to objections by the German Consul as its anti-Nazi theme was deemed unfriendly to a (then) friendly power. However, the theatre continued to perform that play throughout the duration of the war, in factories, warehouses and even down a mine. In 1967, Australia and the USA were engaged in an almost universally unpopular war. *America Hurrah* portrayed the immorality and decadence of American society due to that involvement.

The three plays dealt with the effect on society of the politics of the USA at the time and the involvement in the Vietnam War. Play 1 is a fugue for eight actors called *The Interview*. The second play is called *T.V.* Both short plays deal with the dehumanising of people who have been stripped of any feelings of empathy and individuality due to the increasing violence and indifference of society and its leaders.

The third and most controversial play, *Motel*, consists of three giant doll-like figures, a man, a woman and a third fairly indeterminate figure. The man and woman indulge in a violent sex act, destroying the set and scribbling obscene comments and lurid sex drawings on the walls, all to the accompaniment of a loud voice droning on as the chaos develops. It is regarded by famed author Norman Mailer as 'probably one of the best one-act plays I have seen. A compelling image of American violence'.

The production was banned because of the alleged obscenity of the play *Motel*. General consensus of opinion was that it was banned at the request of conservative Chief Secretary Ralph Willis, due to its unfavourable depiction of our Allies, the USA.

Shades of 1936 all over again.

The arts community was up in arms. Freedoms were being eroded. A committee of Friends of *America Hurrah* was set up by artists, writers, academics, theatre critics and civil libertarians, and a protest performance was planned. This took place, without interruption and when the third and offending play was staged all hell broke loose. The two giant dolls, at the end of the destruction were to lumber off the stage and storm through the theatre with forceful lights shining into the eyes of the audience. It was a final act of aggression. The two actors were rushed out of the auditorium into the foyer with the police hot on their heels. Capture was thwarted by a line of wharfies and other trade unionists. The offending 'dolls' were rushed into a side room, stripped of their costume, towelled down and then the door was opened to the police who were greeted by about six tall actors, male and female, sitting in their underwear. I was one of them and much laughter prevailed as the daunted police went away, tails between legs. This was indeed a victory over censorship because not long after, productions of *Boys in the Band* and *Hair*, both considered somewhat indecent, were successfully staged without interference.

Another production important to me was Chekhov's *The Seagull*. Director Brian Syron had recently returned from New York and from a long association with the great Stella Adler and her acting studio.

He cast me as Madame Arkardina and I can't think of any other theatre company who would have given me that opportunity. Brian gave me an insight to a way of approaching my work that has stayed with me ever since. As a proud Eora man, his talents and his human rights advocacy were an inspiration to all. Brian died in 1993 but his pioneering efforts for indigenous directors and performers goes from strength to strength to this day.

By now it was 1972, and Australia was in the grip of election fever. After twenty-three years of conservative government, real change was in the air. Gough Whitlam, leading the Australian Labor Party, was our beacon of hope out of the wilderness. We on the left (and in the middle too) campaigned vigorously. During my season of *The Seagull*, at a reception for Greek composer Mikis Theodorakis, I was approached by a politician who was destined to become a minister in a Whitlam government. There was an instant attraction between us and this giant of the left captivated me. A brief liaison followed and then I was contacted by the special branch of NSW police force – the branch concerned with all matters political. A meeting was requested. I can only presume that my friend was under surveillance and that, perhaps, the phone at New Theatre was tapped, because when he was on the campaign trail phone calls were coming to me every day. To the police I feigned ignorance and declined to meet. In light of the impending election, I wasn't about to jeopardise the victory with a scandal. So, I reluctantly called a halt to any further contact with this remarkable man. Would it have gone anywhere? I doubt it. Whitlam was swept into office with a landslide victory and yes, my friend did become a Minister of the Crown and his integrity and principles stayed with him until the day he died.

Thanks to good reviews by critics like Katherine Brisbane and Harry Kippax, I finally engaged an agent and began working in earnest. Radio plays came my way and once again, I was side by side-by-side with some of my teenage heroes. There would still be a long road to travel with many bumps along the way but also a lot of laughs.

I was cast in play called *Bandwagon*. It starred Peggy Mount of British TV comedy fame. She was supported by the wonderful Jacki Weaver, Bernadette Hughson and Bettina Welch. I was to understudy Miss Mount and Miss

Welsh. It was a comedy about a mother and two daughters all pregnant at the same time. Jacki actually was pregnant with her son Dylan at the time and her costume padding become less necessary as the season went on.

Years later, Jacki and I were reminiscing about this show and she told me that that great doyenne of the English stage, Peggy Mount, had said of me, 'Marvellous actress, but she'll never get anywhere, because she's a communist'.

This was not far from the truth.

CHAPTER FOUR

FINDING BOHEMIA

In 1968, while involved with New Theatre, I had joined the Communist Party of Australia. This really was an exercise in futility as people were leaving the party in droves due to the fallout of the period of protest over communist rule in Czechoslovakia – a period dominated by mass dissent and demands for liberalisation and subsequent invasion and suppression by the USSR – what would later become known as the 'Prague Spring'. Friendships and loyalties were put to the test within the party as sides were taken for and against the USSR and youthful dreams were shattered.

But back then I was still newly filled with fervour.

Now I didn't exactly wear a hammer and sickle on my t-shirt and call everyone 'Comrade', but I happened to be the representative of our union, Actors Equity, and merely abided by the regulations of the award. Hardly revolutionary!

Being a communist wasn't *that* big a deal. In many ways it was an extension of a whole lifestyle, a way of looking at the world formed from experiences that people who were living 'safer', more conventional lives couldn't necessarily appreciate. We didn't always have that secure, shall we say, middle-class faith that the authorities were on our side or would come to our aid when we needed it.

By this time Kirk and I had moved out of Bondi and said goodbye to the Hungarians. We were now living in Balmain.

While we were in Balmain Kirk gave up the sea faring life to spend more time with us. He took a job as an organiser for the actor's union,

Actor's Equity. This was a calling for which he was well suited as he had a background in trade unionism. Among the many areas requiring his attention was the signing up of new members. It seems that the strippers in the clubs at King's Cross at the time were working in conditions that were less-than-acceptable. The strippers decided that if they joined a trade union, they would have better protection at their place of work. Kirk and his colleague Col Voight visited the girls to hear their grievances about working conditions and began to sign them up. This was not met with good grace by the owners of some of these clubs who were, shall we say, somewhat on the shady side of the law, to put it mildly. On another occasion, Col visited one of the clubs at the invitation of the strippers and was brutally bashed. His injuries were so severe that his spleen had to be removed. This hideous situation then came almost to our front door in Balmain as we witnessed a strange car with tough-looking occupants regularly parked outside our house. This really had me scared and Kirk and I felt that something should be done about it.

Through an old-time resident of the area, we expressed our fears and concerns to the sister of a notorious man who had grown up in the area and, although he was no longer a resident, frequently made visits to his old haunt. That man was the infamous Lennie MacPherson who some have described as one of the most notorious and powerful career criminals of the late 20th century. It is rumoured that he controlled most of Sydney's organised crime activity for several decades. We understood that his sister told him our situation because the unwanted vigilance suddenly and mysteriously stopped. To me, this was an example of the old-time loyalty that inner city suburbs with tough, working-class backgrounds were known for.

Maybe experiences like this, as well as Kirk's influence, might have influenced my decision to become a Communist?

But I think that I joined the party, in the main, due to my growing interest in politics and also because a media branch of the party had been established. I thought that this would consist of people whose literary, political and cultural leanings would make for a stimulating atmosphere. I expected robust discussions on the merits of poets, authors and journalism as it affected our political beliefs.

My hopes of intellectual stimulation were dashed when, at my very first meeting, I discovered that my fellow comrades belonged to the printing industry. A noble calling in and of itself, but not quite what I was hoping for. Roger Milliss from New Theatre was the only *bona fide* author there who was able to expound a little on what I was looking for.

Most of the member's discussions and debates consisted of such earth-shattering speeches as, 'Brothers! Today on the shop floor so-and-so declared such-and-such!' or 'Comrades! We must work harder to secure better factory conditions!'

Admirable stuff, and I understood the importance of it all, but it hardly gave me an insight into Proust, Jean Paul Sartre or Dostoevsky.

Needless to say my revolutionary fervour waned, and I resigned my membership but not my lasting socialist principles, and I guess that the enduring legacy of my flirtation with communism was those socialist principles.

To this day I have the utopian dream of a fair and just society – a place where education and health are upper most in the minds of politicians, a country that cherishes its young and respects its elderly; a place where the indigenous people of the land have a more inclusive and respected place in their own land. Far too slowly I see the powers that be taking notice of scientists in relation the decline of the planet.

We can only hope that it is not too late.

But I digress ...

The late, great Betty Pounder, choreographer, dancer and mainstay of the mighty JC Williamson's Theatres had become a casting director, and in 1974 she cast me in John Mortimer's *A Voyage Round my Father* which was to star Sir Michael Redgrave. It almost didn't come to fruition, as the producers wanted to import an English actor to play Redgrave's son. This was not about to be agreed to by Actor's Equity as it was felt that many a fine Australian actor could fill the bill. At the time I was on the Federal Council of Equity, and although I knew I had been cast in the play, I still opposed the importation.

My heart was in my mouth at the prospect of losing so prestigious a job, but sense prevailed, and a fine young actor was cast. Ironically, Barry Hill was originally from New Zealand, but he fit the bill as a bona fide Australian.

Also in that cast was Jeannie Drynan, who went on to have a stellar career here and in the U.S. Jeannie is fondly remembered as the hapless mum in the hit film Muriel's Wedding. We shared digs on tour and she is one of the warmest, funniest roomies a girl could have. We had a fun time.

To be in the same cast as Sir Michael Redgrave was an honour. His performance was a masterclass in simplicity and control. He was also extremely generous in his support of us younger actors.

On one occasion, he came to my dressing room and said, 'Maggie, you used to get a great laugh on such and such a line. You seem to have lost it, I think I know how you can get it back'. It was simple matter of an emphasis that had softened over the run of the show, something that often happens when one becomes comfortable in the role. It is a common fault among actors and in this case it was easily remedied, and I got the laugh back!

He was right. I took his advice and got that laugh back immediately.

Although becoming increasingly frail with the onset of Parkinson's Disease, he had made the effort to climb the stairs up to my dressing room to deliver that valuable advice.

A true gentleman of the theatre.

In 1975, once again, Betty Pounder was to cast me. This time in a lavish musical, *Irene*. It was to be an extremely successful theatre debut for the delightful Julie Anthony in the title role made famous on Broadway by Debbie Reynolds. I now found myself in a very different world, a world of high glamour, high kicks and high comedy. It was to be directed by Freddie Carpenter, an ex-pat director who had carved out a successful career in the UK Kenneth Rowell designed the most breathtaking costumes, glorious visions of silk chiffon, furs, velvets and glittering jewels – all the extraordinary high fashion of the Art Deco era. It was a feast of glamour and I loved every minute of playing a snobbish, wealthy New York matron. I didn't actually sing the song I did with the debutante chorus – it was deemed more effective done in a recitative manner, that is spoken lyrics but in perfect time with the melody.

Many friends were made during that season: Nancye Hayes, Tony Geappen, Jack Webster, Doreen Warburton and a young dancer named Karen Johnson. Karen would go on to play such roles as Cassie in *A Chorus Line* and carve out a wonderful career as performer, teacher, choreographer and director. Thirty-five years later we were reunited when Karen stepped in to become resident director on *Wicked,* and it was a joy to be working with her again. Karen had married Steven Mortimer, one of the all-time greats of Australian rugby league and although I found the combination of football and showbiz intriguing, it certainly works for them and many years of happiness have been enjoyed.

Noel Ferrier played the flamboyant Madam Lucy with all the outrageous aplomb that only a wit such as he could do. Unbeknownst to me, he and my friend Tony Geappen had a running gag going. Each night, Tony would pop a note under Noel's door with the name of some diva. One night it might be the great Edith Evans, another it might be 40s star Virginia Mayo with a turn in her eye, or it could be any old idiosyncratic showbiz star. The purpose of this game was to try and make me crack up. It was all to no avail as I remained stony faced for months. Then one night out of the blue, I looked into Noel's face and burst out laughing. He was completely nonplussed as he hadn't been given any instructions from Tony that night. The cause of my merriment was a smudge of eye makeup that gave him a decidedly lopsided look. Perhaps it was a case of 'small things amusing small minds' or maybe it was the hysteria that sometimes comes towards the end of a season. Sort of stir crazy, in fact. However, I eventually regained my composure and carried on. Noel was a wonderful company man. It was no secret that for many years he had struggled with alcoholism. To his eternal credit, prior to joining the *Irene* cast, he had gone along to AA. Those meetings continued wherever we were and for that entire season, Noel never missed a performance nor gave any sign of even a sniff of alcohol. He was funny, friendly and full of life. The refrigerator in his dressing room always had champagne chilling for visitors.

I marvelled at his strength of character and had enormous respect for him.

So, in spite of Peggy Mount's prediction that I would 'never get anywhere,' I was working, which for an actor in Australia in those days, *and even in these days*, is really saying something.

Twenty years later when I was on a personal appearance tour in the UK I met up with dear old Peggy, playing the Fairy Godmother in a pantomime.

She gushed and said, 'My dear Maggie, I always knew you'd make it!'.

Bless her!

*   *   *

It's a common topic to recount where you were when major events happened. When JFK was assassinated, I was a newlywed and preparing breakfast. When 9/11 happened, I had dozed off in front of the TV and woke up thinking that some late-night disaster movie was playing.

One of the most significant events in my lifetime was 'The Dismissal'. A popularly elected government led by the great Gough Whitlam was sacked by the then Governor General, Sir John Kerr. This was particularly galling to those of us who had voted this government in because, since their election in 1972, they had changed the face of Australia forever. Out of the stodginess of the fifties and sixties, we were now out there for the world to see.

I was on tour in *Irene*, at the time, we were playing in Brisbane. Many of us had digs in a suburb of that city and being sub-tropical, and summer, we rejoiced in the presence of a swimming pool. At 11 am on November 11, 1975, we were happily lying around the pool, with the radio playing the pop music of the day. Then came the interruption broadcasting the ghastly news. Instead of taking to the streets, or a general strike, the anger and pain of this action seemed to manifest itself more in deep sadness and disbelief.

And it wasn't just governments. As the seventies progressed, my marriage continued to fall apart too.

Who is ever to blame in such situations?

Was it my absences touring? Was it my perceived infidelity?

Was it his alcoholism?

No doubt I enabled this aspect by not realising just what an illness it was. Too many times I had matched him drink for drink and then some, never realising that this was simply adding fuel to the fire. Violence had crept into our dwindling relationship and that was too hard to bear. The uncertainty of the mood I would find on my return from the theatre, the outbursts, the hidden bottles, the bruises and the tears, the running with Caitlin to friends' houses for sanctuary. By 1978 our fifteen years together was over, and we went our separate ways. I always maintain that twelve of those years were splendid and that his early influence, love and support was immeasurable. Besides, without those years, I would not have my Caitlin and, for that alone, my gratitude to him is boundless.

In the end, to put things in perspective, and to be fair, my fifteen years with Norman Kirkpatrick weren't all alcohol, accusations and violence.

The first twelve years were among the most productive and exciting years of my life thus far. Along with welcoming a beautiful child into our lives, my confidence as an actor grew thanks to his support and encouragement. We enjoyed many happy times together. Our mutual love of books, politics, food and people enriched our lives immensely.

Among the many stimulating people who came into our lives was Tas Bull.

Tasnor Ivan Bull was Kirk's oldest and best friend in Australia. They had met on the waterfront in Tasmania when both were working as wharfies. Their mutual politics cemented a life-long friendship. Tas moved up high in the echelons of the trade union movement. After moving to Sydney and working on the wharves he was elected Vigilance Officer in 1967. I am fondly reminded of this event because I helped his election campaign by posting up 'Vote 1 Tas Bull' on pylons and poles around the Darling Harbour precinct. This historic part of Sydney was once known as 'The Hungry Mile' because during the Great Depression, unemployed men queued along that stretch looking for work, *any* work that they could get. By the late sixties, with the depression a not-so-distant memory, the area was a busy, industrial working port of Sydney. It's still a busy place today, but the port is now all gone and has become the famed Barangaroo site – as indeed have many of the wharves around Sydney due to the containerisation and mechanisation of the industry. Like Kirk, Tas had been a member of the Communist Party but he left in 1959 following the suppression of the Hungarian revolution by the USSR. He was responsible for radical changes in the workings of the waterfront, having risen through the ranks to the position of general secretary of the Waterside Worker's Federation. He then went on to become Vice President of the ACTU – The Australian Council of Trade Unions. From 1972 onwards, he worked with the International Transport Workers' Federation and for ten years was on the executive board of the Asia/Pacific region.

Having said all that, the Tas Bull I knew and loved as a loyal friend was not all serious politics and trade unions. He loved good food, good company and a good time. It would be remiss of me not to mention his place in our lives, as his presence was as important in my life as it was in Kirk's and Caitlin's. Unfortunately, when Kirk and I separated, my contact with Tas and his wonderful wife Carmen diminished. I regret that loss of contact but at least I had fifteen years of a most wonderful friendship. When he died in 2003 aged 71, I was deeply saddened but all the better for having known him.

CHAPTER FIVE

LIVIN' IN THE SEVENTIES

In 1971 I was invited to take part in a post-graduate course at NIDA, the National Institute of Dramatic Art. This course enabled eight actors, four graduates and four non-graduates to spend several months receiving tutelage and workshopping two new Australian plays. These plays would be performed at the Jane Street Theatre. Set in an old church in eastern-suburban Randwick, the Jane Street Theatre was a small venue – it seated fewer than 100 people – but it was meant to be a place to show new works and indeed it was the birth place of many new Australian works including *The Legend of King O'Malley*, *Terra Australis* and the legendary David Williamson play, *Don's Party*.

Under the guidance of such tutors as Peter Carroll for voice, Keith Bain (who would later choreograph me in *Songs from Sideshow Alley*) for movement and Rex Cramphorn and Bryan Nason for acting and improvisation. This was a time of fresh beginnings in the art of acting and methods such as Jerry Grotowski's 'paratheatre' were being introduced. An avant-garde area of theatre, like Stanislavsky before him, Grotowski would revolutionise modern acting techniques. Among his many experiments were attempts to blur the line between performer and spectator. His mantra seemed to be 'poor theatre' and often foregoing the use of props altogether, it allowed actor's bodies to represent different objects, establishing an intimate dynamic between actors and spectators.

It was a wonderful experience and introduction to the world of improvisation and inventiveness. I personally felt that I gained considerable insight into what makes an actor tick by being there.

The first of the two new plays we workshopped was *Truth*, a truly dreadful play about the notorious newspaper baron Ezra Norton. Despite the talents of highly skilled director Aubrey Mellor it was unplayable and unsalvageable.

I am happy to say that I have had very few hideous plays to deal with. The averages have been pretty darned good.

The Ripper Show, for example, while not quite a disaster was in fact a fun show to do. It was on the double bill with the successful and weirdly titled, *Don't Piddle Against the Wind, Mate*. *Ripper* was about a travelling vaudeville family, presenting their particular brand of theatre across Australia in tents, local halls and country theatres. It was set in the time of the Jack the Ripper murders in London. Into the company of this happy band of players comes a mysterious stranger. The fertile imaginations of the family run riot as they try to figure out just who this man is. The result is a chaotic romp as they try to set traps for him, all the while totally convinced that he really is Jack the Ripper.

But all actors at some point, sometimes at several points, during their careers have to put up with bad shows. One simply can't spend as long as I have in the theatre and not have some shows that are best forgotten.

Among my memories of the odd dog productions, *Truth* is a real standout. *Truth* missed every mark of what makes a play work. It was the story of Ezra Norton, a notorious newspaper owner of the ghastly *Truth* newspaper, a scandal sheet and a forerunner of today's equally grubby tabloids. The play tried to be stylised and innovative but despite the efforts a talented cast and director, it missed the mark enormously.

Another production I later worked in was *Social Climbers* – another virtually unworkable play. A group of women on a hiking trip, stuck in a mountain cabin, and under the influence of much wine disclosing all manner of secrets and foibles. It all sounds rather promising *in theory*, but *the reality* was a mess. Once again, the director, the highly talented Babs McMillan, and a terrific cast including Belinda Giblin, Paula Duncan and Fiona Press failed to make a silk purse out of this sow's ear.

Other plays such as *We Find A Bunyip*, *Up a Gumtree* and *Pirates at the Barn* are memories happily lost in the mists of time, along with a really strange dinner theatre show with a title that I tried unsuccessfully to repress – *How I Stuffed an Ostrich for the FBI and Found God*.

In contrast to the disaster that was *Truth*, the second play of the Jane Street season was a different story altogether.

Childhead's Doll, by Ralph Tyrell and William Young, was known as a 'pop opera' and had been developed in their home town of Brisbane. Brian Nason directed us, and it was an experience never to be forgotten – for all the right reasons, I hastily add. It was a beautiful and uplifting piece of theatre – gentle, whimsical and utterly satisfying to play.

One of the many highlights of my time in this course was a visit to Parramatta Prison. We were a privileged, small group of theatre people invited to witness something that would soon explode onto the stages of Australia.

Jim McNeil, the playwright, was serving a seventeen year sentence for armed hold up and shooting a police officer. McNeil was a career criminal who had spent most of his life in and out of prison. While in Parramatta he joined the Resurgent's Debating Society and subsequently wrote his first play, *The Chocolate Frog* – prison jargon for 'dog'. It was this play that we were taken to see.

Walking into that cold, unforgiving Victorian prison was daunting. The clang of the gates, the coldness of the guards and the chill one received from simply being there made for considerable discomfort.

We were ushered into a smallish hall and seated in front of a small stage with a shabby floral curtain strung across on wire.

The curtains opened and the play began, performed by the inmates. These prisoners had a raw, vital quality about their performance. What it may have lacked in finesse was made up for by the honesty and passion they brought to their roles. We were moved and excited by what we had been privileged to witness. There was some brief socialising over a cup of tea and then it was time to go. On leaving that imposing and somewhat scary place, I felt, as the doors clanged behind us, that there was something barbaric about locking people away in that fashion.

My feelings on that day were a far cry from the time in the future when visiting my criminal acquaintances inside became the norm.

McNeil went on to write *The Old Familiar Juice* and *How Does Your Garden Grow?*, plays that are performed to this day. He was released from prison on parole ten years early due to the intervention of Sydney arts identities. On his release, he became the darling of the theatre scene, but it seems that his life on the outside and, in the rarefied air of celebrity, his talents as a playwright seemed to be devoid of the stimulation that had helped create his earlier successes. He died of alcohol related illnesses in 1982.

That evening we all went to see a professional production by the Old Tote Theatre Company. A cultural shock after our uplifting experience of earlier in the day. As I sat and marvelled at the slickness of performance and the sophistication of the production I couldn't help but compare it with the earthiness and honesty of theatre in the prison.

* * *

Throughout the seventies I was privileged to work in some very fine productions with exciting, talented people.

Among some of my favourite productions were two plays produced in Adelaide for the State Theatre of South Australia. These were *Farewell Brisbane Ladies* and *The One Day of the Year*, both directed by Kevin Palmer. Over the years Kevin has become a much-loved friend and for a time in my career he was my agent.

Farewell Brisbane Ladies, written by Doreen Clarke, saw me teamed up with Monica Maughn. This hilarious play is about two old prostitutes meeting up after some time 'off the game'. Monica's character has retired into suburban respectability but her old friend Winnie (whom I played) is as loud and blowsy as she ever was. She invades her fussy friend's domain with her outrageous behaviour and causes hilarious chaos all the way. It was a slight piece, but it gave me great pleasure to exercise my comedy 'chops' and to share the stage with Monica. Mon was one of the finest actors of her generation with an enviable record of fine work. Sadly, no longer with us, she was much loved and admired.

The One Day of the Year, Alan Seymour's iconic play, explored the family turmoil over the relevance of Anzac Day. This play resonated with me because the conflict between the father and son was akin to the conflict that has been between my stepfather and me. The teenage boy in the play and teenage me questioned the 'glorification of war', as we saw it. It took me some years to realise that that is not the case. The reverence afforded that day is in memory of those who had made the supreme sacrifice and it is a sentiment embedded in the soul of my country. The role of the mother, which I played, was reminiscent of my own mother, trying desperately to keep the peace.

Every actor has a nightmare story.

There are the nightmares we have when we are asleep, the scary sort such as walking onto a stage armed with character and dialogue only to find that you are in the wrong play. Or the one where you should be at the theatre, on stage but you can't find your way to that theatre. Obstacles are all along the way.

These are just two of the scary ones of the many that I have experienced during the course of my career and they usually come during a rehearsal period or a production week when opening night is looming. Sometimes they can be quite pleasant dreams or even a little erotic such as falling in love with the leading man. Although, I admit, with most of the battle-axes I have played, romance has (usually) been a long, long way off.

We have our onstage nightmares too. The small glitches like a 'dry' which is a momentary forgetting of a line and then quickly having to improvise in order to keep up the flow of the play. Or the props that aren't in their correct place, or the door that won't open or shut or the telephone that rings when it shouldn't or doesn't ring when it should.

There is a theatrical legend of a production where a telephone rang at an inappropriate moment. The actors on stage were frozen with fear, none more so than a very young actress at the start of her career and nervous enough as it was, let alone being confident enough to be able to rescue a scene. The star of the show, and I believe it was some one of the stature of a Dame Edith Evans, wafted across the stage, picked up the phone and turned to the trembling young actress and grandly said, 'It's for you, dear.' Now that is a hell of a nightmare for an ingenue.

One of my most terrifying moments did indeed occur during the Adelaide season of Alan Seymour's classic *The One Day of the Year*.

It's the final scene, Anzac Day over, tension is still high between the father and son played by Peter Cummins and Tom Burlinson who have just had an almighty row about the relevance of Anzac Day.

Dad: seated at the kitchen table nursing a beer, anger and a hangover.

Mum (me): about to make yet another pot of tea to calm the situation.

Son: rather downcast after the argument and the departure of his girlfriend.

The scene is very quiet and still.

At this point Wacka, the old family friend played by Bill Austin, is supposed to enter and lighten things up. At the expected moment ... no Wacka appeared.

I began to improvise madly with Tom about all manner of things from cups of tea to the weather to his girlfriend to the imminent arrival of Wacka.

For an agonising period of time – probably no more than five minutes but that's a *lifetime* on stage – the banter between us continued. Finally, I said, 'Watch the kettle will you, love?'. I excused myself and ran like hell across the back of the stage to the dressing rooms where the stage manager was finally rousing Bill from a little afternoon nap! I then raced back to the stage, took a deep breath and sauntered back onstage and rinsed my hands as if I had been to the lavatory. I made the pot of tea and finally Bill walked in and the play could finally end.

During all this time the audience was absolutely hushed.

Looking back, I am sure they were holding their collective breaths as the play is so well known they would have wondered at this new ending.

Then curtain call – lights up, applause, lights down – and my knees buckled from under me and dear Tom had to hold me up.

Adrenaline had gotten me through but there was always a comedown when the crisis is over!

Another play around that time was Patrick White's *A Cheery Soul* directed by Jim Sharman – a superb production which featured flawless performances all round, and especially Robyn Nevin as the ubiquitous Miss Docker. Miss Docker, an iconic Patrick White character, has been played by several fine Australian actors, but it seems that Robyn Nevin is the one most remembered for her remarkable performance of the meddling, pathetic Miss Docker. I played several roles, but my favourite is Mrs Lily, a wistful old woman in a nursing home, sitting apart from all the other old women, lost in a reverie of her first love. Through a haze of dementia, she maintains a sad dignity.

Another Patrick White experience was a film *The Night the Prowler* also directed by Jim Sharman. The film starred Kerry Walker and Ruth Cracknell. My small but interesting role as Ruth Cracknell's best friend allowed for some wry comedy. Not a monumental film or role, but one I enjoyed immensely, especially as I was once again directed by Jim and it gave me a wonderful moment with Patrick White on set.

It was a night shoot, and in the wee small hours we shot a scene that Patrick wanted to watch. Apparently, it was to hear me utter one of his favourite lines, which was:

'I met a divine Communist once. He was a plumber. Came to fix my pipes and stayed to indoctrinate'. When I delivered this line, there was a huge guffaw from behind the camera. The Nobel Laureate had given a sign of approval.

It wasn't my first film, but previous roles were so inconsequential that my memories of them have been lost in the dusty recesses of the past. Films like *FJ Holden*, *Lilian's Story* and *Encounters* are on the list of films that didn't exactly have Hollywood calling.

Another important film early was *The Getting of Wisdom* directed by Bruce Beresford. It is a delightful coming of age film from the novel by Henry Handel Richardson. I think it is a beautifully crafted film and it still delights today. Thanks to Google, I was astounded to find that the budget for the film was AU$525,000 – one of the examples of fine Aussie film making of that era.

* * *

In 1976, along with actors Felicity Gordon and Kit Taylor, I was engaged to workshop three one-act plays with students at the University of New England. Colin George, an English director had commissioned the plays.

We were housed in very good digs on campus and Felicity and I set up house along with my daughter Caitlin whom I had enrolled in the local school for the duration.

One of the students taking part in the venture was a local lad whose father owned a turkey farm.

He was an unassuming, polite, handsome, country lad who, it seemed, had no particular desire to be an actor. He was just doing some sort of BA (I don't remember specifically) and the drama course was just a part of it. He seemed to think at the time that working on a prawn trawler would be a dream job.

However, he possessed an extraordinary talent. It was a gift that I would have hated see go to waste.

I *urged* him to take his talent further, to study, go to drama school, *whatever*, but not to let that potential go.

On my return to Sydney I contacted John Clark, then head of NIDA – The National Institute of Dramatic Art – and implored him to send an application form to the student in Armidale.

This he did, the young man was accepted into NIDA and the rest is history.

The young man I begged to become an actor is the great Philip Quast who has enjoyed an astonishing career over the past forty years both in Australia and in the UK where, among his many awards, are *three* Laurence Olivier Awards, the most of any actor to date.

One of the plays written by Ron Blair was about the breakup of a relationship between two bibliophiles. A most acrimonious split that involved the separating of their vast collective library.

As the tensions built, so too did the language.

Felicity was playing the woman involved and, as I was busy learning lines for my own play, she called upon Caitlin to hear her lines. Bear in mind that my daughter was ten at the time and as it progressed Caitlin, reading the man's part, came upon some pretty hefty swearing. In fact, the whole play was peppered with more F and C bombs than even I had ever heard before. Cool as a cucumber, Caitlin read on and every time she came to an F or C word she would simply say 'beep' or get 'beeped' It made for a less than interesting version, but I felt it showed some ingenuity on my daughter's part.

Another highlight of our Armidale stay was the fact that it was winter, and I saw snow for the first time. My own particular adventure happened one evening when I went to take a shower. As there was no air conditioning and the night was cold, I turned the shower on. With no thought to water waste, I let it run so the bathroom filled with steam and was warm enough to strip off in. This I did and was enjoying a most wonderful hot shower when the door burst open and in rushed several burly firemen. I know we have all heard of melodramas involving firemen and damsels in distress, but this just wasn't one of them. A hasty retreat from the red-faced men and a contrite apology from me. The glorious steam had set the fire detectors off.

Juggling life between theatre and film is something we actors dream of, but it is not without its cost.

In my case I feel that it partially contributed to the end of my marriage, and the absences from my daughter play on my conscience today.

At the time, I didn't think too much about being a working mother, I am ashamed to say. It probably seemed to outsiders that I was single-minded, selfish and ambitious. Perhaps I was but I also had reasonable support from my mother who periodically took over the motherly duties and had Caitlin stay with her in Newcastle and attend school there. I like to think that during the periods when I wasn't working, our lives together were as normal as any other mother/daughter relationship. I have friends who were selfless enough to put their careers on hold – in particular work that involved touring – while their children were at school. On reflection, If I had my life to do over again I would do things *very* differently. However, there isn't much point dwelling on that issue and Caitlin seems to have turned out all right.

A more light-hearted interlude at this time was a drag show! Yes, I have done a drag show. My good friends David Mitchell and David Penfold occasionally wrote shows for the highly-patronised drag scene of Sydney. These witty, camp, satirical shows had voices recorded by professional actors and then the script was mimed by the drag artiste. On this occasion, the production of *Cinderella* had lost one of its ugly sisters and, at the last minute, I stepped in. What a crazy time this was. The cast was heaven sent, David Williams a.k.a. Beatrice was the very unlikely Cinderella, Ronne Arnold was the wicked stepmother, the elegant Corinne, the fairy godmother and my dear friend Lyn Lovett was Buttons. My old friend from the Kings Cross days, Carlotta, was alongside me as the other ugly sister. I had known Carlotta (Richard Lawrence Byron) long before her well-documented transition from handsome young man to famous, glamorous star of cabaret, film and TV. To this day I regard her as a dear friend. The whole experience was a crazy, camp romp, even when I forgot to mime ... after all, I wasn't used to another actor's voice coming out of me.

Once during the run of *Cinderella*, we, the cast were sitting in our communal dressing room, clad mainly in undies as it was so damned hot. Carlotta, recently recovered from her pioneering sex change operation, was regaling us with all the gory details. For some reason, she stood behind me making mock, lascivious movements around my nether regions. Bear in mind I was in my bra and undies. Across the room came the laconic voice of Corinne – Fairy Godmother and Wit Extraordinaire – well known for her camp exclamations, 'Carlotta,' she said, 'Leave her alone, her varicose veins will get a hard on!'

This was followed by a convulsing cast falling about at the absurdity of it all. Good drag queens were never without witty retorts.

Along with that delightful sidestep there were other, more serious moments of theatre.

One of which was *Lower Depths* by Maxim Gorky, a dark study of 'down and outs' in a Russian flophouse at the turn of the century. It was directed by famed Romanian director Liviu Ciulei. It was a broad, sweeping production with a large cast of notable actors including John Bell Brian Syron, Kris McQuade and Jennifer Claire. The director spoke very little English, but his directorial skills were not diminished. He managed to communicate with us brilliantly and an exciting, world class production resulted.

Another outing for my Irish accent was a play called *Da* in which I played the wife of Tom Farley (from my early Shakespeare days) and the mother of Tom Burlinson – a pleasure I would have again within the space of a few years.

Then, an all-time favourite came my way. Tennessee Williams' *The Night of the Iguana*! What a thrill this was! Ted Craig directed and in the cast were Judi Farr, Max Phipps and Ronald Falk. How blessed was I to be in such company! Three of our finest. The role I played was Maxine – flamboyant, blowsy and flirtatious, with inner strength and pride.

Happily for me it was the days when I was svelte enough to wear skin tight pants, push up bras, and had a cleavage to match. Ah … days long gone. Our stage manager was one John Frost who went on to become Australia's premier theatre producer and winner of a Tony Award for his production of *The King and I*. John Frost would come back later into my life with *Wicked*.

Deathtrap by Ira Levin was one of the last productions from JC Williamsons or 'The Firm' as it was known. I was cast as Helga Ten Dorp, the clairvoyant, along with Dennis Olsen, Robyn Nevin and, just out of drama school, John Howard. We were privileged to have Michael Blakemore as director, another expat director/actor who had carved out a great career in the UK. Sydney born Michael Blakemore was a two-time Tony-award-winning director, with numerous Drama Desk Awards. He was invited by Laurence Olivier to be one of two Associate Directors of the National Theatre in its infancy. His vast theatrical career extended into film, including his adaptation of Chekhov's *Uncle Vanya* into the very Australian version titled, *Country Life*, which he not only starred in but directed as well. His remarkable life spanned film, theatre and writing. In 2010 he was inducted into the American Theatre Hall of Fame.

Two other productions from the seventies dear to my heart were *Songs from Sideshow Alley* and *The Kenna Trilogy*.

Sideshow was written by Robyn Archer, famed songwriter and cabaret performer. Surprisingly, I was cast alongside my friend from the *Irene* days, Nancye Hayes. For over fifty years, Nance has been a truly remarkable force in the history of Australian showbusiness. From her early days as a member of the chorus in JCW Musicals to starring roles in *Sweet Charity, Chicago, Guys and Dolls, 42nd Street* and many more. She has directed, choreographed, taught and inspired countless young performers. She is a true leading lady and her talents would not be amiss on Broadway or the West End. I am proud to call her a friend.

Being cast beside her in *Sideshow Alley* was a thrill beyond belief. Our chemistry as the two old side show spruikers was magical. We did all manner of tricks – magic, knife-throwing, lassoing, singing and dancing. For the magic tricks, we were privileged to have the great Ross Skiffington coach us. In the hands of this urbane, master magician, we learned the secrets of The Sword Box and a disappearing act. Of course, we were sworn to secrecy and never to reveal the magician's secrets. To find myself beside Nancye doing a soft shoe shuffle was the stuff dreams are made of. Sadly this show, which should have gone further, was in the hands of theatrical dilettantes and their inexperience forced it to close long before it deserved to.

The Kenna Trilogy was the autobiographical creation of Peter Kenna. It chronicled his life first as a boy struggling with his sexuality in an Irish Catholic family, through his experiences as an actor, to his life as a chronically ill playwright.

John Tasker directed this three-play epic which premiered at the Adelaide Festival of 1978.

I was cast in the first play, *A Hard God*, as Aggie, the mother. She was depicted as a tender, stoic woman of great faith – typical of so many Irish Australian women of her generation, devout, loyal and probably, in today's vernacular, a Tiger Mother, prepared to defend her family at all costs.

In the second play, *Furtive Love*, I played Dora Dare, a flamboyant diva of the theatre and in the third play, *An Eager Hope*, I once again played Aggie in her seventies. It was a small cast playing multiple roles – Ray Meagher, Janice Finn, Phillip Ross and Alan Wilson. Tony Sheldon played Peter Kenna throughout the three plays. Vic Rooney, a powerful actor, played several roles including Dan, the husband in the first play.

Peter Kenna died in 1987 and sadly, Vic died in 2002, whilst we were playing in *Singin' In the Rain*.

The seventies were a somewhat topsy turvy decade for me. After my marriage, I embarked on an affair with a much younger man. Perhaps the 'toy boy' was a reaction to my years spent with an older man. Big mistake! Aside from the occasional pleasantries, the major downfall once again was violence. Another violent drunk, who, through whatever insecurities he had in our relationship, manifested itself in raging outbursts.

Intervention by friends put him out of my life. He died some years later in a car crash. I believe that it was as a result of a high-speed police chase. An inevitable end, I suspect.

In between jobs, I managed to acquire a new skill. Thanks to the good graces of Norm Hodgson, owner of the Strand Hotel, I became a somewhat better than average barmaid. A skill that came in very handy when I was between jobs because I still had a daughter to raise and bills to pay.

The Strand was 'The Actors Pub', a meeting place for any of us who might be in the vicinity. A place to meet like minds, hear about jobs or network with radio producers from the nearby ABC studios.

Friday lunches were legendary. Anyone who was there, available and willing would be part of these very long lunches. They were usually held at one of the nearby, cheap Italian restaurants. Casks of red wine and loads of pasta were the order of the day. To finish off a 'cleansing ale' or two was tipsily had back at the pub.

Along the way, I had many small parts in television and films. Sometimes a reasonably substantial role, sometimes what you might call a 'spit and a cough' or sometimes, cutting room floor material.

These parts were few and far between.

I was never really very confident in either medium. So many of my contemporaries had cut their teeth on the multitude of roles in Crawford television productions. Hector Crawford was a pioneer in the world of radio and television. His company produced a plethora of shows such as *Homicide, The Sullivans, Cop Shop* and *The Flying Doctors*, to name just a few. These shows spawned our great array of film actors, directors, designers and producers, so many of whom have had great careers both here and in the USA. A small part of me regrets that I wasn't a small part of the genesis of the remarkable Australian Film and Television Industry.

And as the seventies drew to a close, changes were to come into my life that I could never have imagined.

CHAPTER SIX

PRISONER OF THE EIGHTIES

This chronology of the eighties is likely to be as erratic as my life was in that decade. It all began fairly optimistically but proved to be perhaps the most tumultuous time of my life. Professionally it was very productive, but privately, it left a great deal to be desired.

The Pirate Movie was an absolute hoot. It was a musical romantic comedy and it starred Christopher Atkins, of *Blue Lagoon* fame, and Kristy McNichol, known for *Little Darlings* and TV sitcom *Empty Nest* – two terrific young Hollywood stars. Christopher was such a daredevil, doing most of his own stunts in a spectacular fashion. Kristy was a little more reserved but totally dedicated to her work. Also in the cast were Garry McDonald, veteran actor Bill Kerr and also Rhonda Burchmore. Ted Hamilton was the star and one of the producers along with David Joseph.

The director was Ken Annakin OBE, a most esteemed British director who moved to the United States where some of his many credits included *The Longest Day*, *Battle of the Bulge* and *Those Magnificent Men in Their Flying Machines*. His career spanned over fifty films from 1941 to 1992. It was a real pleasure to work with him. He was an absolute gentleman who managed to get the best out of everyone in a calm, reassuring way.

I just loved the whole experience and on top of being extremely well paid and looked after, it was also a great fun time off set.

New Year's Eve 1981 brought some interesting news.

Ian Bradley, who had returned to *Prisoner* as producer, was casting a new prison officer role. Yes, I watched the show and as an Australian actor I was proud of it. I had originally auditioned for the role of Vera Bennett – Vinegar Tits – which went to Fiona Spence. I gave it no further thought, got on with my theatre career.

A mutual friend, having a drink with me on that New Year's Eve, mentioned that Ian was looking for an actor to play a 'sadistic, corrupt, bull-dyke screw'.

Exact words.

For a reason unknown to me, Ian seemed to think that I could play the part! Never one to shirk a challenge, I jumped at the chance and before long my agent had negotiated the contract and I happily signed for three months – no audition necessary.

Ian and his wife, actress and script writer Annie Lucas, were friends from the acting fraternity in Sydney and the pub life I have already written about. My bar jobs, the long lunches and the camaraderie are what led to Ian offering me the role.

As the world now knows, *Prisoner*, or *Cell Block H* as it was named overseas, was an extraordinary, ground-breaking production that gave international recognition to its almost entirely female cast. Most of the women came from successful theatre careers and throughout the series' eight-season run, created some of the most memorable characters ever seen on television.

It was a hard road for all concerned – the cast and the remarkable crew.

These days I doubt that anyone is contracted for twelve hours a day, five days a week, forty-eight weeks of the year. Two hours of television was made in those five days.

My introduction as Joan 'The Freak' Ferguson was a very nerve-racking one. To walk onto a set of established characters and a cast that had been together for nearly 200 episodes, was daunting – to say the least. I was certainly made welcome but the terror in me caused me to be very still, physically. This proved to be the right move, accidentally, as it gave Ferguson a menacing presence right from the start.

A year or two later John McCrae, who directed my first episode, pointed out that I had lost some of my menace by 'acting' tough, instead of the menacing stillness of before. I had become too cocky and probably a bit lazy. It was a criticism well noted and happily taken on board.

Lines were often learned on the run. That is from scene to scene. I would have my script in my hand for the camera rehearsals then when time came for a 'take' those pieces of paper were shoved wherever, under pillows, in cupboards or under my bum if I was shooting the scene sitting down. This method was perhaps not the norm, but it served me well enough for nearly 500 episodes. In my evenings at home, I would sort out shooting sequence, read through the lines, make any notes I might need, then 'wing' it the next day.

Playing the same character for so long enabled all of us to simply step into a scene and know precisely who we were and what we were doing.

Throughout my four and a half years on the show, I had the privilege of working with some of our finest actors. Among the many, were Val Lehman, a fine opponent of Ferguson's machinations and a fabulous sparring partner, Sheila Florence, a veteran of the theatre and a rather grand eccentric – a legend. Gerda Nicholson, Judith McGrath, who for all the severity of her role was one of the wittiest, funniest women I have known. Her theatre comedy performances were side-splittingly funny. Off the set, we had many laughs and long lunches and dinners. Judith died in 2017 and she is greatly missed by all who knew her.

Elspeth Ballantyne is, to this day, a dear and loyal friend who has never been backward in telling me to pull myself together when the occasion arose. I cherish all my memories of our friendship.

Betty Bobbitt, Tina Bursill and Anne Phelan are three fine women whom I am proud to call friends.

There are wonderful actors, too many to mention, but almost all very dear to me and to whom I owe a debt of gratitude for being so terrific for me to terrorise. Of course, there were some great male adversaries and they include my old friends Peter Adams from the Shakespeare days, Ray Meagher from *The Kenna Trilogy* and Maurie Fields, a much-loved performer from vaudeville to theatre and television.

It was all so new and exciting and although originally contracted for three months, it stretched into four and a half years, over five hundred episodes.

Not only were the actors inspiration for my performance, so were the directors, producers and particularly the crew who guided me through the skills of acting in front of the camera.

To credit just a few of them, I thank Steve Mann, Kendal Flanagan, Mark Piper, Jenny Williams, Ray Lindsay and the incomparable camera crew.

Ray Lindsay, our beloved floor manager ran a tight but friendly studio. Known affectionately as 'Uncle Rabies' he was a man of great integrity, warmth and humour.

Steve Mann, Mark Piper, Sean Nash, Rod Hardy and Kendal Flanagan are just a few of the fifty or so directors who worked on the show during its seven years. All were special in their own way and I learned a great deal from each and every one of them. Some have gone on to bigger things in the world of film and television.

Kendal Flanagan was probably the most eccentric of them all. He was a force of nature and had the makings of becoming a world class film director. He informed me that we had first 'worked together' when as a teenager he operated the follow spot during the Melbourne season of *Irene* at Her Majesty's Theatre.

Kendal was a quirky, somewhat troubled soul, but he lived for his work. He was particularly proud of the fact that he often shot an extreme close up of just my eyes during some dramatic moment. He claimed he felt like Scorsese shooting De Niro in *Taxi Driver*, just the eyes telling the story. His demons, however, were insurmountable and his brilliance was cut short when he died of an overdose in 1999 after a long battle with his heroin addiction.

Anecdotes about *Prisoner* are legion. We all have our own take on the tales of life on the studio set. Although we worked long, hard hours along with the hard work and long hours there was a lot of humour. Not just among the actors but the crew as well. And by the end of a long working week, tiredness would become fatigue and would cause us all to become a little hysterical. Sometimes a fit of uncontrollable laughing caused the odd actor to be sent from the studio to recover. Discipline dished out like this was always done with a smile and the culprit would go outside, have a smoke, and then come back to continue. Jokes and laughter abounded, and I am sure it was because of the nature of some of the intense, dark scenes that a little comic relief eased the tension. Betty Bobbitt, who played Judy Bryant, and Anne Phelan, who played Myra Desmond, were not just great actors dedicated to the job, they could be outrageous pranksters as well. Judith (Colleen 'Po-Face' Powell) McGrath's sharp wit had us in fits of laughter and Elspeth Ballantyne (Meg Ryan) was a notable giggler. Sometimes, very late on Friday afternoon, when the bubbly or a 'cleansing' ale had come out for the last few scenes, hysteria could be rampant. So much so that rumour has it that on one occasion Sheila Florence (Lizzie Birdsworth) laughed so much she wet her pants. I can't verify that but I wouldn't be surprised and I doubt she was the only one that that ever happened to.

PLAYING JOAN – DOING MY OWN STUNTS

Playing a character such as Joan Ferguson entailed a *lot* of physical work. Although for the most part I had to be stealthy and menacing around the corridors I also took part in some extraordinary stunt work. Under the guidance of Glenn Ruehland, our official stunt coordinator, I took part in some stunts that nowadays would *never* be allowed. Insurance companies would have a *fit* if a leading player did some of the stunts that came my way. Notable among them were a 'dream' sequence that required that I be hanged (episode 413). It was very scary in spite of the harness as I could feel the rope tightening around my neck as I released the dead weight of my body.

Then there was the famous fire and fight scene between Val (Bea Smith) Lehmen and me in episode 326. The fight began in the prison set as the fire began to rage and continued to a point where we were trapped and then on to finding an escape route to take us up to the roof top. In the next episode (327) as we made our way up a very steep ladder, Bea was injured and in front of Joan. At that point I lost my grip and fell back off the massive ladder. Although I had a harness on, I swung out and back again, banging my leg on the iron bars of the ladder. It was a good result though because I had swung out of shot and the effect had to be that I had plummeted to the floor below. Mission accomplished!

Another hair-raising stunt was in episode 646. I had to hang from a steep cliff, rescuing, Rita 'The Beater' Connors, played by Glenda Linscott. The process of setting this up was very complicated and scientific. It was to be a stunt that could only be done once, no second takes here. Glen and the camera crew set up the shot, all manner of checks were made – sound, camera, my harness, everything. One last pat on the shoulder from Glenn and over I went. All the adrenalin imaginable pumped through me (and Glenn, too) and Bingo! We had the shot. I can't explain the rush that doing things like that gave me. Sometimes, I think it was better than sex!

Glenn supervised many fight scenes that I had to do and a couple of very memorable ones, aside from those with Val, were with Glenda Linscott, Peter Adams and a very special one with the late Maurie Fields.

Another time I almost gave Glenn a heart attack when after being hit over the head with a breakaway chair, I fell to the floor and stayed there. Glenn really thought that I had done damage that caused me to lose consciousness and almost began CPR! When I jumped up and laughed at his ashen face I felt that I had amply repaid him for all the torture he put me through for four years. He was a great stunt man and a gentleman to boot.

Today, my body is reminding me of all those tumbles taken on cement floors.

Happy to have a little security at last, little did I realise that the bane of my life, my occasional lapses into selfish, arrogant behaviour would, in time, lead to a black hole.

During this time, I was commuting regularly to Sydney where I found myself once again involved with a younger man. This time it was very different. I was surrounded by heroin addicts and petty criminals.

I have no idea what possessed me to become embroiled in this life. I still, to this day ask myself that question. What was I trying to prove? Was it a grossly inflated opinion of myself? Did I see myself as some sort of 'bad girl' from an old forties' movie?

The only thing I do know was that it was a completely destructive chapter in my life and one that I am not at all proud of. At this same time, a friend in Melbourne was also in the grip of heroin. A creative soul who deserved better than this hideous addiction.

I am at a loss to explain my stupidity with the attraction to less than desirable men. It is something that troubled me for a long time. I really have no explanation for it, but I am not particularly proud of some of those episodes in my life.

Eventually, I settled in Melbourne and leased a house in a leafy suburb. My friend Peter Flett, an actor from Sydney, moved in as my house mate.

Here was my chance and inspiration to create in the kitchen. What fun we had. Sometimes, when home at the same time for dinner, Pete would make a martini and we'd chat in the kitchen while I cooked. Sometimes we would simply watch television, shrieking at the antics of Joan Collins in *Dynasty*. He was the perfect house mate and we often say, 'if these walls could speak'. Why?

We loved entertaining and had many a long lunch or dinner with the friends we had made in Melbourne.

I think our front door was the revolving door of fun, although my personal life was somewhat less than fun.

Addicts around me – the previously mentioned Kendal Flanagan and the young person in Sydney – I'll not dignify his existence with the term 'man'. He was an immature, selfish con-artist and I fell for the flattery and the lies. In both cases I was simply trying to help these two out of the cycle of destruction that is heroin. I paid for treatments, medication and rehab. I most certainly drew the line at providing them with the poison. All this was to no avail as I was obviously too naïve to realise that all an addict cares about is the next hit.

The out of control lives of the addicts around me, the punishing work schedule, far too much alcohol and occasional use of stimulants, all destined to cause a crash.

And crash I did, in time.

The eighties continued with me juggling increasing pressures of work, socialising and dealing with two addicts, who in spite of the best intentions continued to relapse.

The dark clouds of 1984 had some silver linings. Caitlin turned eighteen and by this time was making her way in the television industry as a director's assistant. Naturally, I felt that some sort of celebration was in order. I needed to do something special for her. I had exposed her to some utmost dangers during her formative years and the guilt is something I feel to this day.

Miraculously, my girl was made of stronger stuff and through all the hideousness of those years, she came through with amazing dignity and strength.

I hired a private function room at Kinsela's, then a very upmarket and popular bar and restaurant. It was also a great meeting place. It was the sort of place one could pop into and always find colleagues to catch up with. A little like the old days of The Strand Hotel only glamourous. Well, it was the hedonistic eighties and we were about as hedonistic as could be.

At this very grown-up dinner party for my girl, I made a little speech that included the line from a Neil Simon film, 'When I grow up, I want to be just like you'. I meant it then and still do. In spite of me, my daughter is a bright, assertive and creative woman. She has been a remarkable mother to her two children and a fiercely loyal daughter to me.

My friends often asked, 'Hell, Maggie, where did you go RIGHT?' I often asked myself that.

The other bright spot of 1984 was my first trip to Europe.

The security that *Prisoner* afforded me enabled me to travel in relative comfort, something that twenty years earlier would have been way beyond me.

My dear friend John Hargreaves had moved to France and regularly commuted back to Australia for film and stage commitments. He also, cleverly, worked a little in French films from time to time.

John, whom I had first met at New Theatre in 1967 was a larrikin in the Australian sense of the word, a larger than life, talented man. Committed to the fight against social injustices he was vocal in his opposition to bigotry and oppression, particularly the Vietnam War and the plight of indigenous. Australians. These traits formed the basis of our friendship – along with our mutual love of acting, food, wine, music and Marlene Dietrich. His French partner at the time, Vincent, was an agronomist whom John had met whilst filming in Western Australia where Vincent was, I believe, doing some sort of post graduate course.

John and Vincent lived in a village called Monchy-Humières, in the Picardie region north of Paris. Monchy-Humières is an unremarkable village in the Oise department. It is a peaceful, rural part of France. They also had a small apartment in Paris on the Boulevarde de Reully, in the 12th Arrondissment. The Monchy house was part of a vast estate surrounded by beautiful woodland and somewhat in the distance had been the chateau of this grand estate. John's house had obviously once been the gatekeeper's house and was enormous with ultra-high ceilings, original timber beams, polished floors, fireplaces and everything I would have imagined a French country house to be.

My flight over was uneventful except for the wondrous moment when we stopped briefly at Athens airport to refuel. It was almost daybreak and as we took off, the sight of the sun rising over the Acropolis took my breath away.

At last I really felt that I was on my way to Europe. The plane then travelled along the Adriatic coastline over the snow-capped Swiss Alps, all visible from my window.

My European adventure was about to begin, and I felt such an over-whelming sense of excitement and anticipation.

The city apartment was small and everything I expected a bohemian Paris apartment to be.

Up winding stairs, scrubbed almost white, past a lavatory on the landing, which after every pull of the chain brought out a woman from her flat, who then proceeded to scrub. She must have been waiting behind her door for the sound of the cistern, naturally, the primitive 'squat' toilet was pristine. Old, but pristine. The apartment overlooked the tree lined boulevard and the colourful market. Close at hand were all the food shops one could desire, the patisserie, boulangerie, charcuterie etc, etc. All the sounds and smells I had anticipated.

A short walk to stock up on provisions, Saturday morning in Paris. I could hardly believe that I was here. Constant tooting of car horns, bustling people and so many dogs! Even residents of very small apartments seemed to have dogs.

I found myself looking at everyone who appeared to be over fifty and thinking, 'My God, what you must have been through with the German occupation'. I expressed this melodramatic thought to John, who quite cynically shot me down in flames with the retort, 'What do you mean? They were probably collaborators!' Ah, so much for my war time romance movies, à la *Casablanca*.

Soon it was time to take our supplies and head for Monchy-Humières. Along the auto route, there were factories and light industry and the land looked sparse and flat. The road into the village was winding and narrow with little houses cheek by jowl. It was evident that farm workers lived here, worked the surrounding farmlands by day, then home to their little cottages and the local bistro, tabac or bar.

On arriving at Rue du Chateau, we had a light lunch and then took off to buy more produce from the nearby farms. We went to a wine merchant who sold the wine in bulk to be bottled at home. The farm produce we bought had been picked that morning.

My time in France was a feast for the senses. My love for food and history were more than satisfied. Delicious seafood, the likes of which I had never seen so elegantly served in such places as Bofinger with its magnificent décor and the most luxurious of lavatories; the simple foods of Les Halles; a ham roll in a cafe with a glass of wine or the fine dining that is quintessentially Paris.

A stroll along the Seine, suddenly turning to see the magnificent Notre Dame was a breathtaking moment as was the string quartet playing as

I wandered through that cathedral, and the monumental sense of history as I wandered the avenues and back streets.

To stand in Place de la Bastille or stroll through the Tuileries Gardens; visits to The Louvre, The Orangerie, and The Pompidou Centre.

To marvel at the Picassos, Matisses, the Impressionists and the old Masters.

To sip Ricard Tomate in Les Deux Magots or Le Café de Flore.

Ricard Tomate consists of 2 parts Pastise, 1 part Grenadine or Pomegranate syrup over ice and topped with a splash of water. Just fabulous on a hot day!

So we'd sit there with our Ricard Tomates imagine all the 'bright young things' of the 20s and 30s doing just that. Hemingway and F. Scott Fitzgerald scribbling away as perhaps Zelda danced on a table or perhaps as Gertrude Stein chatted away to Alice B. Toklas.

See what I mean about the senses and the imagination? Or perhaps it was just the influence of the Ricard Tomate?

Visits to the theatre sadly failed to impress. While looking for the passion that I was led to believe existed in the French arts, I was bitterly disappointed with *Berenice* at the Comédie-Française and with the opera *Medea* at Theatre Champs Elysees, both rather pedestrian and lacking the fire I expected.

Of course, a visit to Père Lachaise cemetery was a must with the tombs of such luminaries as Jim Morrison, Oscar Wilde, Chopin and Abelard and Heloise. I was most touched by the simplicity of the last resting place of one of my idols, Edith Piaf, simply laid to rest with her daughter under her birth name of Gassion.

The post-war monuments to the resistance fighters and to the millions lost in such places as Buchenwald and Auschwitz are extremely moving in their dramatic starkness.

Greater minds than mine have fallen for the charms of Paris and although I have never returned, not one part of its beauty, noise and grandeur is ever far away from my thoughts.

Also unforgettable was a trip to Compiègne and the grand palace built by Napoleon. One couldn't help but feel a little shiver of excitement when confronted with the monogrammed chairs. Just the simple 'N' embroidered on the back of a chair set my imagination going. Purely and simply the effect of being surrounded by so much history, whether a simple chair in a palace, or walking the cobble-stoned alleys and streets or standing where the Place de la Bastille once stood, history was all around me.

Visits to the usual galleries, The Louvre, Musée d'Orsay, L'Orangerie and of course, The Pompidou Centre with it's almost comical exterior which, to me, looked as though the plumbing was on the outside.

A visit to a Picasso exhibition was breathtaking and one particular painting had John and I in fits of laughter. It was a painting of a very blowsy woman, hair tousled, skirts hoisted up and pissing in the gutter. It was so full of life and defiance and John remarked how like a mutual friend back in Sydney it was. Our friend had been known to partake of this particular method of relieving herself with no nod to convention, or the law!

The Armistice Museum and Memorial is something of which I was not aware. I have looked upon memorials to two world wars all my life, but this was something else. Here in a forest in the centre of land where so many were slaughtered was a very sobering sight. There is the massive Alsace Lorraine Monument, the statue of Marshal Foch and the railway carriage in which the Armistice was signed on November 11, 1918 at 11.00 a.m.

The museum itself holds artefacts that attest to all who fought in that war to end all wars.

I took a short break from France to visit friends in London, this too was a wonderful first experience. London is such an accessible city and, like Paris, one in which to walk around and soak up the history, although in 1984, the food wasn't much to seek out and celebrate.

I stayed in Clapham with Dallas, an old friend from my Kings Cross boarding house days and her husband Max. They met me at the airport and whisked me out of the city for my first English pint in a 15th century pub. My time in London was spent doing all the usual things people do on a first visit to that great city.

Christmas shopping at Harrods, seeing some West End theatre, among which was a production of Congreve's *The Way of the World* with Maggie Smith and Joan Plowright; afternoon tea at Fortnum and Mason, the National Gallery, the British Museum and the Victoria and Albert Museum – all frantically crammed into a whirlwind visit.

I even managed to fit in a day trip to Brighton. This was just months after the bombing of the Grand Hotel and the IRA assassination attempt on Margaret Thatcher. In spite of the bleak winter weather, Brighton managed to still charm with its famous pier and splendid Victorian and Georgian architecture, its glory somewhat faded in places but nonetheless it was still elegant. The Royal Pavilion with its magnificent combination of Chinese and Indian influences was a testament to the excesses of pleasure enjoyed by King George IV, a most hedonistic gentleman, I believe.

My fun-filled socialising in London concluded with a visit to the ailing Sir Michael Redgrave and his wife, Lady Rachel. Possibly, the most memorable moments of my time in that city.

We chatted about family, his recent filming of *King Lear* with daughter Vanessa and he chuckled at the thought of me playing Joan Ferguson and all that the role entailed. We dined on a simple lunch of smoked cod, mashed potatoes and peas with a white sauce – very English, I thought. It was a privilege to meet his wife, renowned actress Rachel Kempson. When I said goodbye to Michael, Lady Redgrave walked with me to the King's Road where she implored me to return soon. Sadly, that was not to be – Michael passed away three months later.

Christmas Eve and then back to Monchy-Humières for my first European Christmas. No snow, but much festivity, fun and food. Such delicious food – foie gras, oysters, duck, plum pudding and copious quantities of Moët et Chandon.

Christmas Day was very leisurely with a gentle stroll through the woods of the estate with all its hidden treasures, statues, a grotto and water features all heavily encrusted with moss but nonetheless beautiful. We were also able to pick wild mushrooms and water cress from the little streams running through the grounds. Shots rang out in the distance and we realised that hunters (or poachers) were on the trail of the deer in the forest. A hasty retreat back to the house was in order. So, my time in France was over, and it was on to Italy and my excited anticipation knew no bounds.

From Charles de Gaulle airport, I flew to Pisa, then an hour-long train trip to Florence and the Pensione Annalena. Nowadays it seems to be a very upmarket hotel, back then it was simplicity itself. Rather rustic in appearance but with that old-world Italian charm in its décor – tiled floors, heavy wooden beams and large comfortable furniture. In its previous life it had been the Palazzo Annalena and in 1919 it became a pensione. Situated across the River Arno over the Ponte Santa Trinita. Easy walking distance to all the sights and a little down river from the fabulous Ponte Vecchio.

Here was another feast for the senses, beauty and history. How I adored the Boboli Gardens; the treasures of the Pitti Palace; my first sighting of 'The David' and the magnificent Pieta and the heart-stopping beauty of the Four Prisoners in the Accademia Gallery! They had been commissioned to form a grandiose subject for the tomb of Pope Julius the Second. Due to a shortage of money the project was abandoned in 1506. We are left with the breathtaking image of four men seemingly trying to escape from the confines of the enormous blocks of marble. It provides a moving image of beautiful male bodies striving to be free.

Three wonderful days of Raphaels, Rubens, Titians et al. The Uffizi Gallery and the Duomo.

Talk about a kid in a candy store. All this and amazing food and the promenading of so many elegant people – vastly different to nowadays and the uniforms of 'grunge' that seem to be de rigeur for backpackers the world over.

With head and heart spinning from this Tuscan wonderland, I took a slow bus trip to Siena. This was a great way to appreciate the countryside as opposed to whizzing along the Autostrade. The rolling hills, farm houses and villages perched on hills overlooking miles of gnarled grape vines, slightly dotted with snow, gave me a true peek at Tuscan countryside.

In Siena, more churches, the Piazza del Campo, fortunately not during the time of the twice annual horse race through the medieval streets.

Sunday December 30 was extremely cold and almost everything was closed. I was, of course, able to find some delicious food. Italians don't let anything get in the way of 'mangiare'.

Then New Year's Eve was upon me. Just more wandering around soaking up the charm of this ancient city and a wander through the Duomo. A solo dinner in a deserted but very smart restaurant. Great food, of course, but dining alone on New Year's Eve is rather pathetic. Naturally, as I was leaving the restaurant, the happy party goers were arriving to celebrate Nuovo Anno.

Ah, well then, back to my hotel, some champagne and saw 1985 in whilst watching Maggie Smith in an Agatha Christie thriller and, of all things, *The Godfather*. I'm sure that my intake of bubbly gave me more delight in that favourite film for seeing it in Italian. Cosi e la vita.

New Year's Day (Buon Anno) and a train to Rome. Straight to Via Sistina and the Hotel Internazionale – so close to absolutely everything. Right near the Spanish Steps, near the house where poet John Keats died. John Keats, a major figure in the time of Romance poets such as Shelley and Lord Byron, died of tuberculosis in Rome in 1821. His bedroom is preserved as it was at the time of his death.

Designer shops; piazzas and cafes – more heaven for this Italophile.

I visited the famous Harry's Bar and sampled several *Puccinis*. A *Puccini* is Prosecco with a dash of mandarin juice. A *Bellini* is Prosecco with a dash of peach puree and I presumed that, as it was wintertime, the mandarin was easier to come by than the peach, which would feature more prominently in the summer.

Naturally, a visit to the Vatican was in order even for this old agnostic and after all the churches I had seen through France and Italy thus far, it was still a thrill to see St. Peter's, the daddy of them all.

Interestingly, when I would return to Rome nearly thirty years later, it seemed almost impossible to enter without tickets and queuing for hours (or days). In the winter of '85, I simply walked in. Many hours spent in that amazing place from the catacombs up to the rooftop and the extraordinary views of Rome and the statuary on the roof and inside the dome way above the High Altar, a vertigo making experience. All this with no tickets, no barriers and no crowds. Bliss!

Of course, a visit to the Trevi Fountain had to be made. All those years ago seeing the film *Three Coins in the Fountain*, and so with the title song ringing in my ears I headed for the Piazza de Trevi.

There was no hope of throwing a coin in, it was surrounded by Japanese tourists, so a glimpse of the fountain over their heads was all that could be mustered. Anyway, coin or no coin, I did return.

So, to da Vinci Airport and homeward-bound.

In spite of the inspiring beginning, 1985 was to prove an exceedingly ugly and trying year.

CHAPTER SEVEN

THE YEAR I WOULD
RATHER FORGET

1985 – a good year to forget.

My life spiralled out of control. Of course, I should have been the one to change all that, but somehow, I seemed to be on a treadmill of work, play, substance abuse and an agonising private life.

The two addicts at the core of this situation continued with their destructive lives. One in Sydney, in gaol, and the other in Melbourne on a merry go round of rehab, relapse, rehab etc.

Surrounding us all at this time was a frightening realisation that many of our friends who had exhibited flu-like illnesses were in fact more seriously ill. The little-known HIV was moving on to what became known as AIDS.

We watched helplessly as friends and loved ones succumbed and drifted away from us. Sometimes, they faced death with anger, sometimes with dignity. In many cases they were shunned by families and in the early days often by health carers. Ignorance and fear abounded. Slowly, the realisation of what the world was facing forced authorities to listen and act. Organisations began to crop up to care for the sick, to fund research and to promote public awareness. To this end, Australia led the world in the fight against HIV/AIDS. The Bobby Goldsmith Foundation, The Aids Trust of Australia and ACON were just a few whose tireless work began to turn the public's perception of the disease and in many ways alleviate the prejudice that existed.

There was still a long way to go and in fact it wasn't until the 21st century that treatment and awareness raised the survival rate, to the extent that some people have lived for many years managing the disease. My involvement with fund raising continued on into the late 1990s.

* * *

Now and then during the punishing schedule of shooting *Prisoner*, I would take myself off for a short break to ease the frantic pace of work and the dilemmas of my private life.

One such break would be to take a week and go to Warburton in the Dandenong ranges outside Melbourne. Here, at the Adventist Health Centre I would embark on a Spartan routine to cleanse the body and the soul. It was totally vegetarian, no tea or coffee and definitely no cigarettes and alcohol. My week would consist of 6 am hikes up a mountain, and it was usually winter when I was there, so the experience was … bracing. Breakfast, then a different type of massage every day, a workout in the gym, a swim in the pool, a short rest in the afternoon and then another hike before dinner. Consequently, will all of this vigorous and healthful activity, I would be asleep by 8 pm. This tough but invigorating regime perked me up no end. I would return to Melbourne, glowing and fit. The effect didn't last long but it was great while it did.

Another memorable break was going to Port Douglas over an Easter break.

I had such good intentions!

I had booked into a seaside motel, stocked up with healthy food and lots of videos, absolutely intent on a getting as good a rest as possible.

Well, so much for the good intentions.

I discovered that there were a number of people from Sydney living the tropical lifestyle up there and, as if in a Somerset Maugham novel, copious quantities of alcohol fuelled that tropical lifestyle. I found myself caught up in a whirl of art openings, parties, restaurants and fast-paced living. It was all terrific, of course, but it did nothing to ease my fatigue. It was pretty much a case of going back to work to give myself (and my liver) a break. One of the highlights of the trip was meeting up with Diane Cilento and travel in her Mini Moke up to Karnak, the extraordinary place that she had developed in the magnificent rainforest area of Far North Queensland. It was an arts centre like no other. An open air playhouse had been built, dwellings surrounded the property that were designed for artists and writers and other creative souls to come, stay and create. There was such a wonderful atmosphere. Diane's then husband, Anthony Shaffer, was also in residence and what a fun man he was. He of course was the noted author of many books and films including *Sleuth* and *Somersby* and he had also written screenplays for *Murder on the Orient Express*, *Evil Under the Sun* and *Death on the Nile*. I found him to be quite eccentric in a very English way. He played a silly game with me at the table that seemed to hark back to the English boyhood penchant for being 'punished by Nanny.' Probably due to the character of Joan Ferguson, I found myself having as ferociously as possible to order him to pass the salt, pass the bread, eat your greens, don't talk with your mouth full etc. It made for a good laugh at the time but later it did make me wonder a little about Anthony's … 'proclivities'.

A real highlight of my time at Karnak was a swim in a mountain pool. High above in the rainforest was a running stream and sitting in it under the canopy of tropical trees was bliss. As the water ran down over the rocks, it created a sort of massage along my spine. The water was unbelievably cool and crystal clear. Although not a religious person I would say that the experience of being in that stream looking up at the sky through the filter of lush trees was as near to being in a cathedral as I could imagine.

I found that these breaks were absolutely essential to my mental and physical health, but the good they did could only go so far.

For my own part at this time, late 1985, I found that I could no longer cope with my life as it had been. 'An empty tank' was how one doctor described it. I never want to experience that feeling again, the feeling that my mind and my body refused to work. You could say that I was almost catatonic.

Thanks to the intervention of my then-agent, the remarkable Bill Shanahan, I was admitted to a private clinic in Sydney. To ease my embarrassment at this move, Bill assured me that there was a well-worn path from his office to that clinic, indicating that I was not the first performer to seek such help. Two weeks of gentle care, mild sedation and counselling, saw me seemingly well enough to head back to Melbourne and work. I have often thought, cynically, how thoughtful of me it was to have a so-called meltdown during a two-week production break.

The rest of the year is somewhat of a blur and then 1986 was upon us.

A most joyous moment in the roller coaster of my life was to meet Sammy Davis Jr.

In the February of that year, he was on a tour of Australia and it is well documented that he was a fan of *Prisoner*, and, as it turns out, a fan of my work.

On arrival in Melbourne, he requested a visit to the set and with great excitement we waited for his arrival by helicopter.

We were filming in the studio at the time and it all came to a halt when he walked in. There was such excitement from all of us. I was like a giddy schoolgirl (and indeed, so was he!). When we met, we both jumped up and down squealing like teenagers at a pop concert. I was incredibly flattered by his attention and his opinion of my performance. He likened it to some of the women in the 'noir' films that came out of Hollywood in the forties and fifties, black and white films that I have always enjoyed.

A group of us were invited to his show and I was especially honoured when he sang 'My Funny Valentine', dedicating it to me ...and it was, in fact, St. Valentine's Day.

After the show, we were treated to supper in his suite, which he had equipped with all the cooking paraphernalia needed to whip up culinary delights. This was, apparently, his after-show ritual – his love of food and the relaxing effect preparing it has on him.

As the year wore on, I had some moments of pleasure in my work but also moments of frustration. It seemed that the writers were running out of ideas for Joan. A few of their story outlines were fairly ludicrous in light of the character that I had created.

Sometimes the writing of *Prisoner* seemed to go a little off track. Occasionally it appeared that the continuity of Joan Ferguson's character hit some confusion. As the person closest to the character and its de facto creator, I felt a responsibility to the viewers and my own credibility, to step in when I saw story lines that didn't quite feel right.

One ludicrous suggestion was that Joan, in her loneliness, take up ballroom dancing.

Well, I really objected to that. I could never have imagined her letting dancing partners into her personal space.

This idea was replaced by having her take up golf. Now, that was an idea that appealed. I thought that when the golf story was finished, I could claim a nice set of clubs for myself and perhaps really take up golf. This idea was thwarted when the set of clubs used were returned to our floor manager Ray Lindsay and went straight back into his garage. So much for any dreams of golfing trophies.

The lesbian affair that the writers came up with was acceptable enough, but I approached it with some caution as I had never regarded the character I had created to be a candidate for love. She was, after all, fiercely ambitious, perhaps too much so to be hampered by emotional attachment. I did, however, comply and I felt that the story was handled with some compassion and dignity by Margo Knight and myself. It was, after all, the eighties and we were yet to reach the explicit portrayals of lesbians in shows like *Orange is the New Black* and *Wentworth*. An interesting point was in the words of the break-up of the relationship. We, the director, Margo and I agreed that the words of heartbreak and lost love are the same, whatever the gender. The hurt is just the same.

I also thought that the storyline of Joan learning to drive a bit silly. Given the character of Joan and her military father, I imagined that she could not only drive like a Formula One driver but that she was more than capable of changing tyres and doing her own mechanical tune ups!

I like to think that any show, television or theatre is a collaborative effort. Each department – acting, make-up, props, costume, directors and assistants – they all need each other to bring together a successful venture. Generally, I have found great support and camaraderie among all those involved in a show. Of course differing opinions will crop up constantly, it could be a performance issue or a costume disagreement, anything really. Sometimes these glitches can become rather fiery and it takes the diplomacy of the director, producer or head of department to smooth the situation. Tensions can run high as a show nears opening night and we are all prone to some excess of temperament and sometimes the first casualty of these mini wars is that the collaborative vibe slips away. But in 99% of cases all ego will be pushed aside for the common good of the show.

The protesting and negotiating about Joan and her life in *Prisoner* brought back some semblance of truth to the proposed storylines but I could feel the urge to leave growing stronger.

Fortunately, the decision was made for me in September of 1986. And in it was decided that production would cease after 692 episodes of ground-breaking television. I was always amused by the term the press insisted on using, 'axed.' To me, that word denotes failure and that is something that could never be said about *Prisoner*. There was enough time for the writers to come up with closure for all the stories and for the characters, so 'Successful Conclusion' would be more apt, I should think.

PRISONER

Fate decided that *Prisoner* would remain a phenomenon, and it is now considered a 'cult' classic. I like to think that this means that it has an enduring fan base.

Although, in my head, I'm all the roles I've played, not just Joan Ferguson, I am nevertheless extremely proud of my work in *Prisoner*.

Fortunately, because of opportunities that the Internet provides – opportunities that did not exist thirty years ago when the show ended

– dedicated fans have taken excerpts from the series and have kept the series alive.

I will admit to being a luddite, but I know that the more technologically inclined among you might like to reminisce, so here is a collection of some of Joan Ferguson's finest moments, as can be found on YouTube.

PRISONER YOUTUBE VIDEOS –

SOME OF JOAN FERGUSON'S GREATEST HITS

Prisoner ran for eight seasons for a total of 692 episodes – first broadcast on Channel 10 on 26 February 1979.

Joan Ferguson first appeared in episode 287, in season four in 1982, and her last appearance was in the last episode, 692, on 11 December 1986 – a total of 405 episodes.

Watching all 692 episodes would require 31,117 minutes, or about 518½ hours.

Joan Ferguson's Introduction (Episode 287)
   www.youtube.com/watch?v=Q23a37AkWmk

Joan Bashes Chrissie (Episode 296 and 297)
   'There are lots of things I'd only be too willing to tell the court.'
   www.youtube.com/watch?v=Pt-IkdikGTU

The Gloves Are On – The Freak's Midnight Walk (Episode 323)
   www.youtube.com/watch?v=Jhl0oOJmHSg

Joan Gets Attacked (Episodes 323 and 324)
   www.youtube.com/watch?v=6ViTk8j7sPo

Joan Taunts Bea (Episode 324)
'You weren't much help to Donna Mason, were you, Smith? Or your *own* daughter for that matter.'
www.youtube.com/watch?v=dDQIsVSjUXc

Joan Taunts Bea – Again (Episode 326)
www.youtube.com/watch?v=-l1kSTJ9iOY

Joan Fights Bea During the Fire (Episode 326)
www.youtube.com/watch?v=_qwVmuPYLpc

Bea Fights Joan (Episode 400)
'I can name it after your daughter – "The Debbie Smith Fund for Hopeless …"'
www.youtube.com/watch?v=wcoCtgkRuVk

Joan and Bea's Final Scene (Episode 400)
www.youtube.com/watch?v=LD6Db-4m32Q

Joan's Acid Trip (Episode 413) www.youtube.com/watch?v=sTqU0echwTU

Joan Taunts Stevens About Her Dead Baby (Episode 435)
'But Nicky's dead, isn't he, Stevens? Poor dead Nicky.'
www.youtube.com/watch?v=QNsJVWJb23o

Joan and Len Murphy (Maurie Fields) Brawl (Episode 507)
www.youtube.com/watch?v=nw_0pZtWAJw

End Game of the Ferguson / Murphy Saga
Part 1 – www.youtube.com/watch?v=2u-HJc-A02c
Part 2 – www.youtube.com/watch?v=yLvaLj9XOlM

Joan Beats Up Ruth (Episode 544) www.youtube.com/
  watch?v=srlNNxcAcHc

Joan and Joyce on Laughing Gas (Episode 655)
  www.youtube.com/watch?v=d0q7olZ2b5c

The End of The Freak (Episode 692)
  www.youtube.com/watch?v=76ZRby9kG6M

The Actor Reminisces – From the On the *Inside Documentary* found
  on *The Best of Prisoner* DVD Box Set released in 2004. MK starts
  at 00:45.
    www.youtube.com/watch?v=ivydVCQ0Mck

Prisoner also got a fair share of send ups. Here's one courtesy of the
great Australian comedy sketch show of the eighties, *Fast Forward.*

Prisoner on *Fast Forward*
  Part 1 – www.youtube.com/watch?v=X7aHTOVDPTg
  Part 2 – www.youtube.com/watch?v=ef4Z0d0WlrU
  Part 3 – www.youtube.com/watch?v=aDvZuSh1nWo
  Part 4 – www.youtube.com/watch?v=AE8_nuzZMul
  Part 5 – www.youtube.com/watch?v=ffJss0Wyf5E

As a matter of fact, there's a whole YouTube channel devoted to
Prisoner – PrisonerCellBlockH95. Although I appreciate the fans'
dedication, the videos are of poor quality, and I'd strongly suggest that
fans buy the DVD collection.
    For the super fan, there is also a whole online encyclopedia
devoted to *Prisoner* – prisonercellblockh.fandom.com

So, as all good things come to an end, the quest was then on for work and my life after *Prisoner*. Within a very short space of time, I had three plays and another television show on offer. Such a luxury had never come my way before, and it sure hasn't since.

My return to the stage was in an Alan Ayckbourn play *Absurd Person Singular* which in cryptic crossword language apparently means 'Silly Me' What a joy this was! A beautifully crafted comedy, a three act play centred on three married couples meeting each Christmas, documenting the changes in their relationships. Being Ayckbourn it has lots of laughs but a fair amount of pathos as the lives of these six people unravel.

And what a cast!

Donald McDonald who played my husband, Kerry Maguire, Barry Creyton, Vanessa Downing and John Stone. It was directed by my dear friend John Tasker. What a time I had! After four and a half years of flat vowels, the beautifully rounded vowels and crispness of the language presented a challenge. So, when offered a crash course with a dialect coach, I jumped at the chance. Working with a dialect coach can be quite rewarding, but in this instance I simply needed a brush up on the rounded vowels and clipped speech of middle-class England, not unlike the accents we all used in our early days in the business. Mostly, though, with accents, I have done my own research and somehow have managed to make a fair go of Irish, Dutch, Middle European, upper class New York, Cockney and Yorkshire.

I was so happy to be back in the theatre and to hear the instant response of audience laughter.

Also, around this time a pilot was shot for a new television series. Don Battye, Peter Pinne and Reg Watson, creators of such shows as *Prisoner, Sons and Daughters* and *Neighbours* had created a light-hearted series called *Richmond Hill*. For me, they created the character of Ivy Hackett and I am eternally grateful for the chance to shrug off the severity of their previous creation, Joan Ferguson. Now I was stylishly dressed and coiffed. I think the best description I can give of Ivy is that she was not unlike one of the *Golden*

Girls characters – perhaps Dorothy as played by Bea Arthur – maybe. The cast consisted of fabulous veterans like Gwen Plumb, Betty Lucas, Ross Higgins and Robert Alexander. My friends from *Prisoner*, Paula Duncan and Amanda Muggleton, were there along with a number of very talented, then, newcomers. There was Emily Symons, soon to find fame as Marilyn in *Home and Away* and Dannielle Carter, fresh out of high school and destined for a fine theatrical career.

Danielle Carter was one of the finest young actors in 1988. She always came to the studio totally prepared. Her script was awash with research notes, moves and motivations. She was super attentive to directions and advice. I am not surprised that she became such a dedicated and disciplined actor.

Some of my favourite scenes were with Betty Lucas. Her scatterbrained character was a perfect foil for my droll Ivy. Our scenes really were reminiscent of a *Golden Girls* episode. I loved the freedom of the comedy moments. When the series finally went to air, it ran all through 1988 and had many top line guest appearances.

Before embarking on that year-long series, at the invitation of Sammy Davis Jnr, I went to Las Vegas and Los Angeles. In Vegas, Sammy was appearing at Caesar's Palace with Bill Cosby. This was an enormous treat. To sit ringside and watch these giants of comedy, dance, theatre and film play off each other. It was a master class.

After the show I was invited backstage where I met Sammy's charming wife Altovise. Bill Cosby insisted he be introduced to the 'Aussie'. This Sammy did, and I was invited into Bill's dressing room for a drink. Sammy went on ahead to prepare supper and I spent a most convivial half hour chatting with Cosby about showbiz, Australia, politics and all sorts of trivial gossip. In light of the current events in Mr. Cosby's life, I can state that there was absolutely nothing but conviviality in his behaviour. He was a perfect host and treated me with great respect as a fellow performer.

Off I went to the Davis' suite where once again, the luxury of his surroundings had been turned into a makeshift kitchen where he could rustle up his after-show culinary delights. As midnight came, Sammy produced a birthday cake and proceeded to sing 'Happy Birthday' to me. Yes, it was my forty-sixth birthday and one I am not likely to forget.

Speaking of not forgetting, a sideline to my Vegas visit was a brief encounter of the amorous kind. Brief, yes but in the luxury of a suite with a curtained circular bed and mirrored ceiling, it was the glamorous stuff that Hollywood does so well.

'With whom?', I hear you ask.

Now, that would be telling. No, it wasn't Sammy or Bill Cosby. Suffice to say it was of *The Bodyguard* kind and a one-night stand to remember.

Next day it was back to LA, and further birthday celebrations at Joe Allen's with some of the 'Gumleaf Mafia' as the Aussie actors were known back then. The late John Ewart was there to celebrate with me. At one point, I boldly bought Lauren Bacall a drink. I had always been a fan. Needless to say, she was completely underwhelmed by my gesture.

Later that evening, it was off to the Davis house in Beverly Hills. I caught a cab and, on the way, chatted to the driver and having seen so many Hollywood movies, I asked him if he was wary of any violence while driving.

'Not at all,' he said, 'Not while ever I have this.' He then produced a bloody great Magnum 357 from the car's console.

On arrival at the gates we were cleared by security and then drove on up to the house. Altovise opened the door and in I went, like a starry-eyed schoolgirl, into the home of a megastar. Yes, it was an opulent house with all the trappings one would imagine, and yet it had a luxurious, comfortable feel about it. The sunken living room, plush sofas, an extremely well-equipped bar with an amusing director's chair with Sammy's Hebrew name stencilled on the back, Shmuel.

There were glass display cabinets everywhere full of treasured memorabilia. Tap shoes worn by Bill 'Bojangles' Robinson, one of the pairs of ruby slippers from *The Wizard of Oz* and a pair of white high-heeled shoes worn by Marilyn Monroe in *The Seven Year Itch*. I had great fun trying to squeeze my size tens into them. Barely got my toes in. Hollywood actors were notoriously small back then. I had to laugh at Altovise's little yappy dogs running around with baby diapers on. I guess it made sense with all that white furniture.

I believe the house had once been owned by Debbie Reynolds and Eddie Fisher and it was where Carrie and Todd Fisher spent their early years.

The night was great fun and a wonderful end to a birthday.

Next day it was back to work in Sydney and Melbourne.

Blood Relations for the Sydney Theatre Company and *Emerald City* for the Melbourne Theatre company were next.

Blood Relations was written by that great Australian novelist David Malouf. It was his first and, I believe, his only venture into playwriting. It was big, bold and writ large. It featured John Wood, Heather Mitchell, Deborah Kennedy and Geoff Morell. Our director was Jim Sharman, a great favourite of mine. He brought to this rather sprawling play a creative touch that only Jim could display.

Blood Relations revolved around a larger-than-life eccentric patriarch played by John Wood and centred around the gathering of family at Christmas. A plot that always seems to be fraught with drama as it often is in real life when families come together. My character, Hilda, was a total enigma – another larger than life character with a fondness for playing solitaire, allegedly a former opera star AND circus performer, all this with a middle European accent. Curious but fun to play.

Although, sadly, not a success, I found it intriguing and satisfying to do.

Emerald City, on the other hand was yet another David Williamson triumph. It had already been hugely successful in Sydney and was subsequently made into a feature film with most of the original cast, including a young newcomer by the name of Nicole Kidman.

For the Melbourne Theatre Company, the cast consisted of Jacki Weaver, Peter Carroll, Gary Day, Genevieve Mooy and Gerard Maguire. What a great group of talented, good people!

We were directed by John Sumner in what was to be his last production for the MTC, which he had originally created in 1953 as The Union Repertory Theatre Company, based at Melbourne University Student's Union. To this day the MTC has been at the forefront of presenting new Australian plays.

The Summer of the Seventeenth Doll by Ray Lawler was its first major breakthrough in this area.

I had long wanted to work at the MTC and in particular with John Sumner. That chance came, late, but at least it came. I absolutely adored playing cynical, brittle Elaine alongside those wonderful actors. Elaine – literary agent, world weary and somewhat acerbic in this sharp satirical play about two entertainment industries, film and publishing. The moral dilemma of 'art versus money' was a key point to this Williamson classic.

CHAPTER EIGHT

THROUGH A GLASS, HAZILY

1988 is another year best forgotten. I am somewhat amazed that even through the alcoholic haze of that year, I can still remember it.

Well most of it.

Richmond Hill demanded quite a hefty schedule but for the most part it was very enjoyable. It was interesting to be in such a diverse cast and as I have already mentioned I had a fun time playing Ivy. Although, I must admit, the constant wardrobe changes and make up checks drove me batty after those years of The Freak's one drab costume and drab face.

My private life, once again, was a mess. Seemingly, I had once again embarked on a relationship that proved to be toxic. Co-dependent, excessive drinking led to violence and once again the cycle began. The shouting, the punching, the tears, the apologies and the forgiving ... over and over.

Along with this came bankruptcy. For the years I had been doing *Prisoner*, I had not paid income tax. This was due to my stupidity in accepting at face value advice from fools. I was led to believe that by registering a business name, I would be exempt from tax at source. This I did without consultation with experts in the field. I was also extremely irresponsible and didn't put aside for the rainy day. So, when the tax man came calling, it was a deluge.

I had no assets to speak of except a new car that had been wrecked by the violent boyfriend. So off I went to the insolvency consultant. The wrecked car paid his fee, I surrendered my passport and bankruptcy was declared.

For three years I had to keep and did keep a meticulous record of all income and expenditure and monthly presented these documents to the consultant. After three years, the slate was wiped clean and I had worked constantly during that time, paying taxes up front and providing all the documentation needed.

In 1991, I was discharged from bankruptcy and have been extremely diligent in that area ever since.

The axing of *Richmond Hill* I found to be a relief as I had tried to juggle far too much. The violence, the alcohol and yet another stay in that earlier-mentioned clinic.

It may have been Australia's Bicentenary year of celebrations, but for me it was another year from hell and, to a great degree, a hell of all my own doing.

One good thing to come out of that tumultuous year was a profound weight loss. Nothing like stress to strip off the pounds. Probably giving up alcohol for a considerable time helped, too. It certainly gave me a morale boost to shimmy into a pair of Levi 501 jeans and tuck the shirt *in*. Something that this big girl had never been able to do before.

Also, at this time I was cast in a production of *Anything Goes*. After twenty-six years I was to do another musical.

Anything Goes, is set aboard an ocean liner the *S.S. American*. Reno Sweeney, night club singer/evangelist is en route from New York To England. Also on board is her pal Billy, who has stowed away to be near his love, socialite Hope Harcourt, but she is engaged to a British Lord. Along with these lovesick young people there is gangster, Moonface Martin, and his sidekick Erma, and also Mrs Evangeline Harcourt, Hope's social climbing mother and millionaire, Elisha Whitney. Into the mix are fantastic dancing boys and girls and the comical ship's captain and purser. Not to forget the wonderful Cole Porter songs, *Anything Goes*, *I Get A Kick Out of You*, *Blow Gabriel, Blow*, *You're the Top* and *It's De-Lovely*.

This great Cole Porter classic was being revived all over the world. Here, in Australia, it was being produced by my good friend Mike Walsh and his long-time assistant from his iconic television days, Sue Farrelly was the executive producer.

In the role of Reno Sweeney was the multi-talented Geraldine Turner, a role she was born to play. Hers was a breathtaking performance and when she raised the roof with *Blow Gabriel Blow*, I had goose bumps every time.

Simon Burke, fresh from playing Marius in *Les Misérables*, played Billy. I had known Simon since his days as a ten-year-old coming to acting classes at the old New Theatre in Darlinghurst. Simon, of course, had won awards and plaudits for his performance in the breakthrough film by Fred Schepisi, *The Devil's Playground*. To this day, Simon is a much loved and loyal friend.

Peter Whitford was hilarious as Moonface. Marina Prior, soon to be a triumph in *Phantom of the Opera*, played the ingenue, Hope. Marina was to go on to become an absolute leading lady of musical theatre.

In the role of Erma, the gangster's moll, was the wondrous Jacquie Rae. What a dynamo! Comedy, singing, dancing, acting, the lot and an absolute joy to watch. Jacqui went on to play Reno when we went to New Zealand with equal success.

Along with the ensemble of highly skilled singers and dancers was Grant Dodwell as Lord Evelyn, and veteran performer Tony Geappen from my *Irene* days. Tony had been treading the boards since the age of seven, on radio and on stage with some of our great vaudeville performers.

I had the joy of playing Marina's mother, Evangeline Harcourt, a very snobby New York society matron. My amazing costumes were designed by Roger Kirk and with my weight loss, I felt like a million dollars in such fabulous creations. Roger is indeed the master of glamour.

Even having a silly, fluffy little dog in my arms every performance couldn't take away the sheer joy of doing that show.

Prior to going to New Zealand, I had the privilege of doing another Patrick White play. This was *The Ham Funeral* and I was cast as Mrs. Fauburgus and Robyn Nevin as Mrs Goosgog, two very dotty old eccentrics, not unlike bag ladies, fossicking in rubbish bins and with rather abstract dialogue. I had previously played this role in a radio adaptation of the play. Kerry Walker played the landlady, Mrs Lusty; Tyler Coppin, The Young Man; Pamela Rabe, The Young Girl and Max Cullen, Bob Hornery. Keith Robinson and Arkie Michael made up the rest of the impressive cast chosen by Neil Armfield, and, I understand, approved of by Patrick White himself.

A lasting memory I have of this season is the morning of the first read through. I don't know of any actors who aren't at least cautious let alone very nervous of that first read through. Like new kids in school, we come together, pencils sharpened, eyes bright and rearing to go.

This first read through was particularly nerve-wracking as Patrick himself was there. Frailer than when I had last seen him, and with the ever-present asthma in evidence, he seemed to have shrunk somewhat. Nevertheless, he was there and that was a great thrill. He presented me with a small fan and a funny old ladies' hat from the original 1961 production.

My 'co-old lady', Robyn Nevin, was unable to be there that morning, so when the read through began, Patrick was inveigled into reading her part opposite me. I convinced him to wear the old lady hat and off we went, Patrick with a wheezy, old lady voice and me trying desperately not to laugh.

So, there I sat, with the great Nobel Laureate, frail, and yet loving every theatrical moment of the scene.

It was a moment in time that is firmly etched in memory. Not a recorder, camera or mobile phone to be seen. Just the delicious image. That production was probably one of Patrick's last outings. He died in September 1990.

We filmed the play for ABC TV, and mention must be made of Peggy Carter's make up for that show. It was another example of her make up genius and I for one could not have done without her.

A joyous end to 1989 was a message on my phone when I arrived home from the last performance of *Ham Funeral*. It was December 16 and my darling Caitlin had given birth to her first child, my first grandchild. Our beautiful Daniel had come into our lives and has been a source of great love for me ever since.

As the nineties moved on, so too, did the scourge of HIV/AIDS. By now, so many of us had lost dear friends and loved ones. It is now well documented that performers the world over were smitten by this terrible disease. The lights on Broadway and the West End were constantly going out in honour of colleagues taken far too soon.

Here in Australia, the gay community was in a state of deep mourning and fear as the epidemic took hold. Almost every day there was a new sadness to face. Some of our brightest and most talented were leaving us at an alarming rate. My beloved agent, Bill Shanahan, was one of many to leave us and tragically many more were to come.

Activism became the norm – to seek knowledge, to combat the fear and the bigotry that raged. Homophobia was at its worst. Despite the pain and suffering it was undergoing, the gay community rallied and fought courageously against the odds.

I was very much 'between jobs' and to keep afloat I had taken up work in pubs owned by Dawn O'Donnell. Dawn was a remarkable woman – a larger-than-life character who wore many hats. In her youth she had been among many things, a butcher and a professional ice skater, travelling the world with the glamorous *Ice Capades*. When I met her and her long-time partner, Aniek, she was not only involved in pubs but also sex shops ('adult toy' shops) and steam-baths. She had opened a world of freedom and entertainment for the gay community which was to become world-renowned.

Some people found her formidable; some found her a little scary. Her reputation was varied. Dawn had many friends, some in high places and some in not-so-high places.

She was a quietly powerful and influential person. To me, she was a dear friend and a great supporter of all aspects of the arts. She was a known collector of fine paintings, especially the works of young, upcoming painters. She was a great animal lover and once said to me, 'I don't trust anyone who doesn't like dogs.' I am inclined to agree.

I understand that NIDA, (The National Institute of Dramatic Art) benefited greatly from her bequest when she died. She is greatly missed.

It is to Dawn that I attribute my involvement in the fight against AIDS. Although I was working for a wage in her pubs, she saw the benefit of celebrity. As *Prisoner* and Joan Ferguson had become somewhat of a cult, she set to using that celebrity to raise money for the cause. The perfect way was through the pubs, raffles, appearances, talent quests etc., with me compering.

Thanks to the power of TV we were able to continually raise considerable amounts of money for the various AIDS charities.

A great deal was yet to be done and I found myself not only doing the pub scene but actually working in the offices of The Aids Trust of Australia and the Bobby Goldsmith Foundation, helping to organise events such as Shop Till You Drop, a fun day on Oxford Street where local businesses pledged a percentage of their day's takings. A carnival atmosphere prevailed with notable performers from the gay community entertaining all as only they know how. With lots of pizazz and glitz.

Another fund-raiser was held in the CBD in prestigious stores such as David Jones and Myer. Celebrities from all walks of life volunteered to serve behind the counters and shoppers had the delight of being served by some of their soap star idols, their sporting heroes and even politicians. Once again, the retailers donated a percentage of the day's take. The gay and lesbian community, despite the tragedies within, rallied with their annual Mardi Gras to take advantage of the enormous crowd and raise money.

The first time we did this, a bucket collection, I was on a truck at the head of the parade, leading the festivities and exhorting people to dig deep and put money in the buckets being manned by volunteers along the route. I was alone on the truck except for an elderly drag queen, sitting on a throne and waving regally. The driver of the slow-moving truck seemed to have a heavy foot on the brake, because every time she had to pause, it was done with such a jolt that I pitched forward, megaphone in hand and in danger of joining the crowd below.

Nevertheless, all the activities I participated in over the next few years were not only great fun, exhausting and rewarding, but I was constantly amazed at the love and generosity of the Sydney LGBTQI community.

In January of 1991, I turned fifty. After a couple of splendid 'decade' parties this one was the best. My dearest friend John Hargreaves was back from France and living in a boathouse by the harbour near me in Balmain. At the time, we were both a little bruised from failed relationships, so it was fitting that my milestone birthday was low-key. We celebrated with our mutual friend

Carole Skinner whom we had both known and loved for many years. French champagne, crusty bread and fresh prawns were the order of the day. Three old pals sitting by the magnificent Sydney Harbour. Nothing could be better.

*   *   *

Later that year, I received a fan letter from the UK. This letter was unlike any I had received before. It was written by a young man who possessed writing skills and artistic perceptions beyond his years. His comments about *Prisoner* and my characterisation were completely different to the usual, somewhat banal compliments. It was written as if by an older, established critic of performance.

So impressed was I that I actually replied and thus began a friendship which continues to this day. Robert Cope became my sounding board, my critic and my confidante. Sometimes I think that *he* should be the one writing this book.

As our correspondence continued and the back-and-forth exchanges of favoured video tapes, he suggested that I might consider a trip to the UK to do personal appearances which are very big over there. Plans were made but first money had to be earned.

Fortunately, a play came my way. It was a comedy romp called *Sailor Beware* and had been a huge success for Peggy Mount, whom I had understudied all those years ago in *Bandwagon*. What a fun role! An absolute battle-axe of a cockney housewife preparing for her daughter's wedding, it had the obligatory henpecked husband, the nosy neighbour and the eccentric relative.

Under the direction of Peter Whitford, my then neighbour and friend from the *Anything Goes* days, we had an hilarious time. With me in the cast were Judi Farr, whom I had last worked with in *Night of the Iguana*, Carole Skinner, one of my first and dearest friends in Sydney who had also appeared as Nola McKenzie in *Prisoner*, Jackie Woodburn, also from *Prisoner* and at the time of writing is still playing Susan Kennedy in *Neighbours*.

This was a joyous experience and I loved every mad moment of it.

The trip to the UK was being planned and I was about to embark on my first overseas venture into *Prisoner* fandom.

How the best laid plans etc, etc.

Looking back after all these years, I realise just how naïve Robert and I were.

This was no bells and whistles tour. It was indeed grass roots time. I stayed with Rob and his wonderful mum and dad, Shirley and Ivan, whom I have come to love dearly.

In order to get around to the venues, we were driven by Rob's uncle Peter. So it became very much a family affair.

Through a booking agent, Rob had secured appearances at various venues ranging from working men's clubs, bingo halls and gay clubs all scattered across the West Midlands.

Staying, as I was, in Staffordshire, I was able to see all manner of places from Liverpool to Manchester to Birmingham, Leicester and all points between.

Looking back, I think it was all rather silly and premature. The Joan Ferguson character had only been on air for a relatively short time, so acknowledgement was fairly sparse. London was out of the question at this time. That was yet to come.

Anyway, the die-hard *Prisoner* fans knew who I was and managed to provide me with a reasonable purse to bring home. I did have a lot of fun and more importantly it cemented my friendship with this remarkable young man and his family.

Then it was back to Australia with plans for a return visit.

That came some six months later and proved to be *vastly* different from my previous visit.

What had been a simple, fun, adventure would now become a nightmare.

I was no longer in Rob's capable, caring hands. This time I found myself surrounded by totally inept people, some of whom, below the surface, may have been just a little dodgy.

There was a Prisoner Fan Club person to whom I could not relate at all and a so-called agent who chose to pass monies on to me in a brown paper bag in an anonymous car park. Should I have seen some signs?

'Of course not', she said. 'Who would rip me off?'

Well, think again, Maggie.

The income was sketchy and sometimes a fee was not received.

The time I had spent in a charming country pub was no longer an option, money was running out and I found myself accepting the kindness of a publican and his wife in their pub on the outskirts of Birmingham.

Although I had my return ticket, my passport was being held by the creepy agent.

Happily, I managed to retrieve it. Instead of the lucrative, fun visit of earlier, this one was a disaster from start to finish. I was exploited and literally left in the lurch by a number of interfering people. A far cry from my happier time with Rob, this was a fiasco.

Then, out of nowhere, a knight in shining armour came my way.

Stuart Jarvis is an entrepreneur who had been in contact with the agent who had booked me on the previous visit and, when told of my dilemma, proceeded to find some gigs for me. Celebrity TV game shows and chat shows.

Stuart is a most interesting man and a little bit of an enigma. He is involved in owning art house cinemas, investing in theatre shows, politics and at one stage managed and guided Dusty Springfield through the second phase of her career. He is a kind, considerate and loyal friend and I trust him implicitly.

An amusing example of British bureaucracy occurred at Heathrow as I was leaving. At the immigration desk a rather officious little man noticed that I had overstayed my visa.

'Yes', I said, 'that is correct.'

He got quite excited at having discovered an alien in his midst and pointed out how illegal my situation was. I smiled sweetly and said, 'Yes, sir, I understand your dilemma, but as you can see, I am leaving in an hour, so there doesn't appear to be a problem.'

With that he savagely stamped my passport and I fled, hoping that there wouldn't be a black mark against my name for future visits.

It was now around 1992. *Lend Me A Tenor*, winner of three Tony awards and four Drama Desk Awards, is a crazy, farcical romp about a temperamental opera star, his wife, a social climbing head of The Opera Guild (me), and a side-splitting bellhop, played by my close and much-loved family friend, Peter Rowley with such comedic skills as to be awe-inspiring in its hilarity. Another comedy which also me teamed up with Rowena Wallace, Jacquie Rae, Lyn Lovett, Tony Harvey, and the wonderful Stuart Wagstaff. Gary Down, who could make a statue laugh, was our director.

A great, fun time was had as we toured this show the length of Eastern Australia and some points inland. We went from Sydney as far north as Cairns with our performances in some of the best theatres in the country. I had no idea that such beautifully designed, well equipped, acoustically perfect theatres existed outside the capital cities. Given that we had a lot of travelling, we also had a reasonable amount of down time which enabled us to see the sights along the way and learn a little more of the fascinating natural world of this country. We stayed in hotels and motels along the way and our social life was an added delight to the performing of this fun play.

Stuart Wagstaff, a legend of Australian theatre and television, was almost like a den mother. He sorted our accommodation bookings and made sure that we were a happy troupe. Not a party animal, after the show, Stuart would return to his digs for his favourite nightcap, hot chocolate.

I also discovered another little-known secret about this wonderful man. He actually enjoyed ironing and found it relaxing. Trivial, I know, but a small insight into a man who oozed charm, warmth and generosity and had a most wicked sense of humour. We all adored him. He died in 2015, at the ripe old age of 90.

One of the highlights of the *Lend Me a Tenor* tour was playing in the NSW country town of Dubbo. All country towns hold their own particular delights – especially the warmth and appreciation of the locals. Dubbo was no exception and included in the hospitality was a guided trip to the famous

Western Plains Zoo. This was a treat-and-a-half, especially for an animal lover such as me. We were ushered behind the scenes of this remarkable zoo where animals are housed in environments as close to their natural habitat as possible. The giraffes, rhinos and zebras roam the savannah-type enclosure, tigers are on an island and monkeys swing from tree to tree above our heads. One of the many important breeding programmes is for the endangered rhino. To our surprise and delight we were taken behind the scenes to the rhino enclosure where hopefully they would breed. A curious beast, one came right up to the low fence and I was able to look closely into the great soulful eyes, touch the horn and pat the tough wrinkled face of this remarkable creature. What a thrill!

These images have stayed with me ever since.

Another breeding programme is for the endangered Bilby – a cute little thing, a marsupial native to Australia about the size of a rabbit. We were privileged to not only view these endangered little animals but to actually hold one – avoiding the sharp claws, naturally. Holding a native Australian animal is an experience I would recommend to anyone if they have the opportunity under the guidance of an experienced animal keeper.

On the more human front, my domestic life had changed quite radically. I had moved from the inner city to a rural setting.

This move was with my daughter, her then-partner, Michael, and precious little Daniel.

We rented a large house on 25 acres surrounded by bushland. I threw myself into gardening and discovered a great love for Australian native plants. I soon learned about the surrounding fauna as well and cultivated visits from all manner of native birds.

My education was helped along by visits from my dear mate John Hargreaves and a new chum Craig Bennett. Both were experienced in the ways of the bush and many a pleasant time was had exploring the land around us, the caves where pygmy possums were known to dwell and educating Daniel in the ways of moving rocks to look for snakes. What a wonderful outdoor life this was.

Then, in December of 1993, we welcomed a beautiful newcomer to the family. On December 30 Caitlin gave birth to Megan. From day one she had the makings of an assertive person. As the second child and sister to the 'golden boy' as Daniel was sardonically known, she had to make her presence felt, sometimes against the odds. This she did with great aplomb. Strong-willed, bolshie, lovable and always having to have the last word. She has grown into a splendid young woman, capable and independent.

The very day she was born, her grandfather, Norman Kirkpatrick – Kirk – passed away at home in Victoria at the age of 65.

There was something *utterly*, whimsically Irish about this – one life ending, another beginning – and some of her traits, I feel, can be attributed to him.

CHAPTER NINE

THE THEATRE STILL CALLS

In 1995, I was handed a gift of a role that would be my all-time favourite.

It was the 50th anniversary of the end of World War 2 and playwright John Misto had written an extraordinary play which would win numerous awards and feature on the Australian High School curriculum to this day.

The play was *The Shoehorn Sonata*.

This beautiful piece of theatre writing would play for many years to audiences far and wide.

It is the story of two remarkable women and is based on facts gleaned from survivors of Japanese atrocities. Australian, British and Dutch women. It tells the story of Bridie, an Australian Army nurse and Sheila an English schoolgirl, who found each other after their ships had been torpedoed in the South China seas during the evacuation of Singapore in February of 1942.

Along with other survivors, they were captured by the Japanese and marched to a concentration camp on Banka Island where they endured untold horrors until 1945.

The play centres on a reunion between the two women for a television interview to celebrate the 50th anniversary of the end of the war and we subsequently learn why these two who had survived such unimaginable horrors have been estranged for fifty years.

Of all the wonderful characters I have had the good fortune to play, Bridie embodies all the qualities that I so admire in women of that generation – the epitome of stoicism and old values of decency and loyalty. It was the story of my mother's generation – born during a World War, raised during the Great Depression only, in their prime, to be plunged back into another World War and all that that entails, loss of loved ones, financial hardship and privation when they should have been enjoying a life of love and fulfilment.

Their stoicism, humour and survival instincts, to me, were incomparable. I sincerely hoped that I could honour them.

Shoehorn Sonata has some memorable scenes:

Bridie describing her arrest for shoplifting a tin of shortbread following a panic attack on hearing the chatter of Japanese tourists.

Sheila confessing to having given herself, a teenager at the time, to a Japanese Officer in order to get quinine and save Bridie's life.

The description of starving women being forced up a hill, thinking they were to be shot only to discover a brass band of Japanese soldiers in gleaming white uniforms, playing The Blue Danube Waltz.

We premiered in Sydney at the Ensemble Theatre and I was privileged to have Melissa Jaffer playing Sheila to my Bridie.

We often found many audience members visibly moved by the stories we told and even met an ex RAAF man who had carried survivors out of the camp when the fighting was over. We met many courageous women who had been victims of those atrocities and in every instance, their spirit shone through.

Some ten years later, I was able to reprise the role with Belinda Giblin playing Sheila. We were directed by Jennifer Hagen and the production was produced and toured by the indefatigable Christine Dunstan. How very fortunate I was to collaborate over the years with these remarkable women.

The play was not without its critics and I found it rather peculiar that some theatre companies objected to it on the grounds that it was, in their opinion, racist. I could never come to terms with that argument. After all, the play was depicting true facts from an actual period in our history. I fail to see how it can possibly be offensive to a certain group when the facts are so well documented.

It was also with great pride that I was able to present this play at the King's Head Pub Theatre in London. Once again, I was delighted and privileged to share the stage with a wonderful actress, Susannah York, another great artist who made life a joy to be on the same stage with her.

While *Shoehorn Sonata* was playing in Sydney, across the globe plans were afoot for a production that was not only going to bring me good fortune but new friends and experiences.

Mike Walsh and London producer, Helen Montague, were in preliminary discussions with the creators of *Prisoner*, Peter Pinne, Reg Watson and Don Battye for a *musical* version of *Prisoner*. The show had gathered enormous momentum in the UK and had become very much a cult classic. At the same time, Paul O'Grady, A.K.A. Lily Savage, was having huge success as the host of Channel Four's *The Big Breakfast*, having taken over from Paula Yates.

The plan was to bring Paul and his alter-ego Lily to a stage show on the West End. What that vehicle would be was the question. It transpired that Paul was also a fan of *Prisoner* so, through a series of negotiations, it was planned that a stage version of *Prisoner: Cell Block H*, with music, would hit the West End in the Northern Autumn.

At Paul's insistence and with Mike's blessing, I was to be a part of this adventure to bring the dreaded Joan Ferguson to the musical stage.

I couldn't have been more excited.

But just as all this preparation was going on, also in 1994, I was asked by my friend John Hargreaves to accompany him to Victoria where he was to shoot the film *Hotel Sorrento*.

The purpose of this engagement was to look after John as he was by now succumbing to the effects of HIV/AIDS-related complications. His condition was not publicly known. Although well enough to continue to be the superb film actor that he had become, he wasn't well enough to deal with everyday domestic activities. It was my brief to be a sort of nanny/housekeeper/driver and cook.

None of this was as easy as it sounds. John was a very angry, troubled man at this time. His old rakish, fun-loving self had gone and in its place was a frightened, cantankerous, bitter man railing against the world for the misfortune that had befallen him.

Sorrento, on the Mornington Peninsula, is a peaceful, beautiful, seaside town. The film company had leased a stylish beach house for us and with the car provided I was able to scour the area for the best organic and free-range provisions. That sounds like a dream assignment. On the contrary, it was a nightmare. John was unbelievably rude and demanding. Absolutely nothing was ever good enough and pleasing him seemed impossible. I took all of the abuse in my stride, excusing his out-of-character behaviour because of what he was going through. It was only our long friendship and my love for my friend that stopped me abusing him and walking out.

I did, however, manage to gain some faint praise from him when I cooked a roast dinner for him and his co-star, Dame Joan Plowright. A home-cooked roast lamb dinner with all the trimmings is always a luxury for actors when they are away from home. Interestingly, John was on extremely convivial behaviour that night.

I had a similar experience with him later on when once again I took on the nanny role – cooking, cleaning, shopping and driving. His illness, by now, had progressed and he was enduring some of the debilitating AIDS-related symptoms. As the disease progressed, so too, did his anger. Not just with me but with most of his loving friends.

A lot of John's behaviour during his illness consisted of nit picking absolutely everything anyone did for him. From driving his car, to preparing nutritious, organic meals, or for simply being there. His behaviour was dealt with by we who loved him, but not without some hurt. We understood that his irrational behaviour was based in anger, all-consuming anger. Anger at the medical profession, at the disease and at the world in general. There wasn't much chance that he 'would go gentle into that good night', he would 'rage, rage against the dying of the light' – with apologies to Dylan Thomas.

However horrid he was to me through all of this, in those last weeks before I left for England, nothing diminished my love for him.

The good memories far outweigh the bad – the kindness, the loyalty and the laughter, shared moments of yum cha in Chinatown to assuage our hangovers, fresh prawns and bread rolls and cryptic crosswords, cooking a couple of lamb chops over an open fire in the Royal National Park and eating them without utensils, and a posh supper at the then posh Australia Hotel and Marlene Dietrich.

But as much as I would have wanted to stay and continue to help John, the UK called, and I *had* to answer. Contracts were signed and off I went.

A minor glitch on the way occurred at Los Angeles airport where we had a short stopover for refuelling. Shock, Horror! I didn't have a visa to enter the USA!

The immigration officers went into overdrive and my passport was held and for the short stay in the airport, I was escorted by a security guard until it was time to board my flight. I found all this nonsense quite amusing and may have been a bit mouthy if I hadn't felt so hideous with a ghastly bout of the flu, and felt more like dying than having something to say.

Eventually, we took off and only when we were out of US airspace was my passport returned to me.

I was met at Heathrow Airport by Mike and, thankfully, he had my work permit and so I was admitted to the UK We then drove to the apartment that had been chosen for me. It was a basement flat in Doughty Street, a street that reeked of history. It consisted of Georgian Grade-2-listed houses and while some were private residences, others featured many legal firms and media offices. *The Spectator Magazine*, Doughty Street Chambers, the prominent Human Rights Chambers, Charles Dickens' house where he had written *Oliver Twist*, houses that had been occupied by Vera Britain of *Testament of Youth* fame, Winifred Holby and poet, Charlotte Mew. I was thrilled to be in such an historic area. Added to that was the fact that I was in the Holborn district and cheek-by-jowl to Bloomsbury. Within walking distance was the British Museum, the West End, Soho, Covent Garden and Russell Square.

I couldn't have been in a more stimulating area.

My first meeting with Paul O'Grady was that first night in London. He called by to take me to dinner. Over a drink we seemed to bond immediately. I was drawn at once to his wit and vivacity. My admiration for his enormous talent was to come with the unfolding of our new adventure.

Dinner at The Ivy was something I never imagined myself doing, but there we were in this establishment restaurant, the art deco haunt of celebrities since 1917. Right there in the midst of the theatre district. After dinner, Paul took me on a tour of Soho and some of the livelier bars. It was a laugh-a-minute until the wee small hours and cemented a terrific working relationship and friendship.

Then Monday morning came and with it the first day of rehearsals.

What a thrill to work in the rehearsal room of the Old Vic Theatre! Of course, my imagination ran riot as I thought of all the theatrical legends who had climbed those stairs to make their magic.

David McVicar (now Sir David) of opera fame was to be our director. Interesting choice, but nonetheless a delightful man. Included in that first cast were the wonderful Alison Jiear, veteran comedy actress Liz Smith and Terry Neason.

My dismay knew no bounds when I read the script at that first reading. I found it grubby, offensive and misogynistic. When asked what my thoughts were, I replied without hesitation, 'What time is the next flight to Australia?' I was so incensed. Of course, I knew that it was to be a camp spoof, but I simply couldn't imagine some of that dialogue coming out of my mouth and anyone who knows me is aware of the fact that I am no shrinking violet when it comes to expletives.

Plans were then made to clean it up and for the next few weeks, in fact right up to technical rehearsals, Paul and I along with the cast managed to rearrange the plot and the dialogue to vaguely suit our characters. Even dear Jeffrey Perry, the sole male in the cast playing 'the man from the department', managed to write himself a charming little ditty.

When we moved into the Queen's Theatre on Shaftesbury Avenue for our tech rehearsal, Paul was beside himself with excitement. His dressing room had once been occupied by his idol, Marlene Dietrich. We had many a laugh about her 'presence' guiding him. For me, my dressing room up one flight of rickety stairs typified all that I had imagined in an old London theatre.

I certainly didn't feel the presence of any former occupants, famous or not. Just the occasional wintry blast from the lane outside.

Nearing the opening, Paul was approached by his good friend Sir Ian McKellen to take part in the annual Stonewall Charity Concert at the Royal Albert Hall and enquired as to whether I would also take part.

Would I!?!

So, it was decided that Paul and I as Lily Savage and Joan Ferguson would perform a duet from our soon-to-open the show.

We were on stage with a star-studded cast that included Elton John (in drag) performing a duet with Kylie Minogue; Joanna Lumley and Jennifer Saunders; Eddie Izzard, Julian Clary, Antonio Banderas and a favourite of mine from the late sixties, Janis Ian.

When time came for our number, I delivered my opening line to Lily, already on stage and at the sound of Ferguson's voice, the place erupted. I walked on stage to the thunderous yelling, screaming and booing the villain from 5000 people. It seemed to go on for an eternity before Paul and I could do our number.

What an extraordinary response. I had never experienced anything like it and of course never have since.

Unbeknownst to me, my dear friend Simon Burke (then working at the National Theatre) and Mike Walsh were in the audience and that gave me a warm fuzzy feeling to have known of at least two people in that vast crowd.

So, we settled into getting the show on and despite the inevitable setbacks of setting-up a show, the technical glitches, the script, the running time etc., we had finally opened.

WOW! A West End opening!

Yes, the audience sort of went wild. It was certainly a split audience. Some who hadn't a clue as to what was going on and some who shrieked and applauded at the recognisable send up of the plot, such as it was.

Yes, there was a standing ovation. Apparently, Sir (as he was then) Andrew Lloyd Webber also stood but according to my spies looked rather puzzled by what he had just sat through.

A rough, bawdy over-the-top show. Perfect pre-Christmas fare for grownups.

The critics, in general, were kind and reviewed it precisely for what it was.

'An absolute hoot' – *The Guardian*

'There is, in short, a riot going on in Cell Block H and connoisseurs of kitsch would be mad to miss it' – *The Daily Telegraph*

'A barnstorming spin-off with a pastiche of every pop style from R and B to Gospel' – *The Sunday Telegraph*

Some included such comments as 'the amazing Maggie Kirkpatrick' and 'Lily Savage the biggest blonde bombshell since Marilyn Monroe'.

And, naturally, some of the reviews were not so kind ...

'Maggie Kirkpatrick has the singing voice of a bullfrog, only she's taller!'

But for the most part we were actually blessed with the reviews we had. Negativity was rare and in the main it was accepted for what it was, a silly, camp, night of pantomime-like theatre.

Now I was really settled in London. Almost feeling like a genuine 'luvvie'.

Life was full of fun.

Eight shows a week and plenty of daytime leisure to explore London.

Nights after the show were certainly fun-filled, or should I say fun-fuelled. Soho was our stomping ground and I certainly had a willing accomplice in Paul. There were late suppers at the Groucho Club and *far* too many drinks at the famous Gerry's Club which was run with great welcoming Irish charm by Michael Dillon. Michael and his wife Alison soon became dear friends and often we socialised away from Gerry's at some of Soho's fine restaurants.

Gerry's Club was a fabulous meeting place for actors, writers and assorted eccentrics. I met so many interesting people there, including Keith Waterhouse, the great author of such classics as *Billy Liar*, *Whistle Down the Wind* and innumerable plays, books and TV shows.

Another lively haunt was The French House pub just a few doors up from Gerry's. Another watering hole that had a thrilling history. After the fall of France in WW2, General Charles de Gaulle escaped to London where it is rumoured that he formed the Free French Forces and it is also rumoured that he wrote his rallying speech, 'A Tous les Français', in the French House pub. Throughout its history it has seen among its patrons, Francis Bacon, Brendan Behan, Lucien Freud and it is believed that an inebriated Dylan Thomas once left a rough copy of *Under Milkwood* under a table. It was an unpretentious, interesting pub which is rumoured to sell more Pastis than anywhere else in the UK. Perhaps, I helped that statistic along a little.

Just before Christmas, I was approached by some fans who were nurses at the nearby Middlesex Hospital to draw their Christmas raffle. I very happily accepted their invitation and thus developed a brief but rewarding acquaintance with these wonderful people and their patients in the AIDS ward of that hospital.

Some nights, after the show, instead of cavorting around the town, I would take myself off to the hospital, have cups of tea with the nurses and spend a little time at the bedside of some of the patients who, sadly, rarely had visitors. To be in the presence of these brave souls was reward in itself. To talk with them, to hold a hand as they faced death with such dignity was a humbling experience and is a memory that lives on.

Sadly, during this period, back in Australia, my dearly loved friend John Hargreaves also succumbed to that dreadful disease, having endured it for the best part of ten years.

I had spoken to him at Christmas time in 1995 and they were our last words together.

My sadness was profound, especially being so far away from his family, of whom I was very fond, and our mutual friends. Respite came in the form of four wonderful people. Mike Walsh, Simon Burke, expat actor Ken Shorter, and Philip Hedley who had befriended John while directing in Sydney in the 70s. These four angels met with me at The Actor's Church, St. Paul's in Covent Garden, where we quietly sat, separate yet united in our sadness as we contemplated John's life.

Their presence was of enormous comfort to me. Afterwards we went for morning tea and laughed and cried over cups of tea with stories of John in our lives.

To this day, I wonder where his extraordinary talents would have taken him. At the time of writing, I am seventy-eight years old, John would have been seventy-three. I wish he were here, throwing his head back to let go that great big laugh of his, sometimes being an absolute shit of a man and sometimes being the kind, funny friend whom I adored.

Prior to taking the musical on a National tour, due to help from my new London agent, Gavin Barker, we managed to have a production of *Shoehorn Sonata* presented at the King's Head Theatre Pub in Islington. The pub is a typical old-style English pub however in 1970 Dan Crawford became the landlord and converted the back room into a theatre.

It became a prestigious fringe venue, run on a shoestring budget but with enormous love and enthusiasm. Many plays were tried out at the Kings Head, and many transferred to the West End or even off Broadway. One such play was *Da* which I had played back in the days of the Old Tote Theatre. Hugh Leonard's play not only transferred to off-Broadway but eventually onto Broadway itself. Many established actors had trod the boards at this funny old backroom theatre and now I was sharing that stage with Susannah York.

The play was reviewed quite well, although I felt that some of the younger audiences didn't fully understand its emotional impact. That impact was not lost on older members of the audience. For some, the memory of the war was still sharp and, in some cases, painful.

Susannah was an absolute joy. She captured the essence of Sheila beautifully and actually had a slight genteel eccentricity about her – a very English trait. I was very fond of her. When we closed she was off the next day to Israel to protest at the incarceration of a political activist who was a friend. She was a talented, beautiful and committed woman.

The first tour of the UK in 1996 was a ripper. We travelled from Brighton in the south to Aberdeen, Edinburgh and Glasgow in the north and all points in between.

We once travelled from Swansea in the west to Newcastle in the East, in a stretch limousine.

What a hilarious journey that was! Much champagne on the way and stops at roadside cafes had a jaw-dropping effect on the locals at the sight of the limo and its passengers. Never one for half measures, that was Paul.

It seemed like party time wherever we went. We were greeted with such enthusiasm by the fans across the country. We played in huge theatres most of the time, several thousands in the audiences.

I soon realised the power of television over there. The very mention of *Prisoner: Cell Block H* had queues lining up for tickets. Added to that of course was the immense popularity of Paul's Lily Savage.

It was an amazing experience to travel the length and breadth of the UK and see places I had only read about or seen in movies – castles, stately homes, museums and art galleries – such a feast! In amongst the partying and the frivolity, my love of history was also being stimulated.

Of course, the tour had to end, and it was time to go home. Besides, I needed a rest, perhaps even a de-tox.

Plans were being made for another tour in 1997, so the fun would begin all over again.

Meanwhile, I was back with my family, my garden and the chores that that entails when an amazing offer came my way.

Stephan Elliott, film director of *Priscilla, Queen of the Desert* fame, was about to start work on his latest project. It was to be called *Welcome to Woop Woop*. Enquiries were made as to my availability and subsequently, I was cast as Ginger, wife to Rod Taylor's Daddy-O. What a thrill!

Rod Taylor had left Australia many years before and had carved out a stellar career in Hollywood. Some of his notable successes were, Hitchcock's

The Birds, *The Time Machine*, *Raintree County*, *Giant*, *Sunday in New York* and *The Vips*. His amazing career crossed film and television from the mid-50s to his last film, Tarantino's *Inglorious Basterds* in 2009.

Some of his leading ladies had been Jane Fonda, Maggie Smith, Tippi Hedren, Doris Day, Bette Davis and Rita Hayworth. Imagine my excitement and nerves at the prospect of joining that illustrious list.

I needn't have worried. Ginger was a fun, over-the-top character and Rod was a generous and inventive colleague. We had a ball!

Woop Woop was an absolute romp and became somewhat of a cult classic.

Some of the reviews summed it up:

'An outrageous black comedy.'

'If you're not Australian, you may not get it.'

'One of a kind.'

'Bizarre, funny, definitely worth a look.'

I think one could take those comments several ways.

Nevertheless, it was a dream job.

Shooting took place in the Northern Territory and while we were accommodated in the air-conditioned splendour of a hotel, our location was something else.

Situated about an hour's drive from Alice Springs, the town of Woop Woop had been constructed, tumbledown, fly ridden, and surrounded by red dust desert. This was 'our town'.

So, began one of the most fun-filled, gruelling jobs I had ever had.

Along with Rod, there was Susie Porter, Dee Smart, Richard Moir, Jonathon Schaech (imported from the USA), Dave Hoey and Jan and Bob Oxenbould. Jan is a dear friend to this day.

The cast also included a long list of very high-profile show-biz luminaries in cameo parts, all shot on other locations.

Despite the 50-degree-Celsius heat, the flies and the dust, I really had a great time.

Often on the way back to the hotel in the early evening, we would stop at some of the ancient sights to witness a full moon rising over the desert and illuminating these sacred sights – a spine-tingling experience.

Once back at the hotel, having washed off the red dust and eaten dinner, we gathered around the pool, swam, chatted and drank. The consumption of VB beer was something to behold.

One evening when everyone else had retired, just Rod and I were left to finish off the night.

What then transpired is something that has caused great mirth whenever I have told the story.

Imagine, if you can, a balmy tropical night, full moon casting a magical light on the palm trees and the pool and a man and a woman of a certain age sitting at a table covered in empty beer cans.

He: 'You know, Magg, twenty years ago, I would probably have asked you back to my room by now.'

She: 'Come off it, Rod, twenty years ago, you and I would probably have been through half the cast and crew by now.'

He: 'Yeah, you're probably right. Oh, well, we'll just sit here and talk about my crook hip and your hormone replacement therapy.'

What a guy!

The shoot continued with occasional side trips to surrounding water holes. Crystal clear, sparkling waters with vast red cliffs rising above. It was heaven to swim in these ancient places.

Soon filming came to an end but not before I'd had my head shaved. Yes, it was a bold move on my part, but I couldn't bear the discomfort or the look of a 'bald' wig, no matter how well makeup genius Cassie Hanlon made it. So, with teeth gritted, breath held, I took the plunge and Simon Zanker stripped me of my locks.

I have to say it was absolutely liberating and if I say so myself, my old head wasn't too bad a shape. Make-up and earrings became the norm for me during the regrowth time.

Of course, make-up and wigs are par for the course for an actor.

Make-up to an actor is an integral part of the performance of the facade. Sometimes no make-up is required and that is a most liberating thing. Mostly, though, the application of make-up is a ritual. It is the time of preparation for the performance, a time to reflect and quietly take in the persona about to be seen on the stage. Along with costume and props, make-up is in many cases the icing on the cake of the creative process. Be it a glamourous face, an old face – although as the years go by that *particular* look requires less and less make up – a bizarre face, a face with prosthetics, it is all part and parcel of inhabiting the character. Sir Laurence Olivier was renowned for excessive prosthetic make up and I believe spent many hours in front of the dressing room mirror creating a persona.

Prior to filming *Woop Woop*, I had been approached by Geoffrey Williams and Michael Freundt to do a one-woman cabaret at their legendary Tilbury Hotel. A scary proposition but we agreed to go on with it. Given that *Prisoner* had been such a hit, it was planned to present it during the Gay and Lesbian Mardi Gras. With my past involvement in the fight against HIV/AIDS and the popularity of *Prisoner* in that community, it was considered to be an optimal time.

So, *The Screw is Loose* was born. David Mitchell writing, Andrew Ross music directing. Given that I have never considered myself a singer, but an actor who sings (when pushed), it was very ambitious to tackle a show with some sixteen or more songs interspersed with chat.

Our rehearsals were always fun and productive, and Andrew gave me new-found confidence in tackling the songs. As we approached opening, we called on the talents of Nancye Hayes to fine tune it. This she did with a minimum of fuss and a maximum of class. Her keen eye and finesse gave me an edge that I would have been lost without.

We opened the show to very flattering and generous reviews from the mainstream critics.

One small blot came from the local gay newspaper, *The Sydney Star Observer*. It seems that the reviewer was offended by the fact that I was not gay. Apparently, he found my banter about gardens, grandchildren and domestic life quite tedious. Although a very small part of the show, it was nevertheless my life and that, after all, was what the damn show was supposed to be about.

To add insult to injury, some nondescript journalist from the grubby *Telegraph* newspaper, went so far as to write a follow-up to that critique with his own take on my show. I have doubts that he had even seen it. He actually wrote a libellous piece that claimed, 'She has passed herself off as a lesbian in order to gain an audience'. So much for some people's imagination. Of course, in today's litigious society, I would have had great grounds for legal action. In fact Ita Buttrose, who had once been editor of that paper, advised me to sue. I chose not to. Interestingly, I have not heard of either so-called journalists since.

It has been an ongoing issue in my life, this question of sexuality. Countless times I have been asked that intrusive question. Playing a lesbian on screen is called *acting*, that is what I do. Often my answer was to query whether, Anthony Hopkins was asked if he was a cannibal, given his success as Hannibal Lector.

My friends in the gay community were incensed by these ridiculous writings and as it was Mardi Gras time with lots of late-night entertainment, my good friend Garry Scale, whilst emceeing a late-night cabaret had me stand on stage with him, brown paper bag over my head and he sang the song from Cabaret, 'If you could see her through my eyes.' At the conclusion of the song which originally has the line, 'She doesn't look Jewish at all' he whipped the bag from my face and sang, 'She doesn't look gay at all!' It brought the house down and metaphorically gave the finger to both articles and their writers.

The Tilbury season was a success and sadly, was the last show at what had been the showpiece of cabaret life in Sydney for many years.

For me it was a liberating experience and a delightful memory I have cherished ever since.

Soon it was time to pack the bags again and head off for another tour of the UK with Lily Savage and the gang from *Prisoner: Cell Block H, The Musical.*

This second tour from March to June of '97 was as crazy and successful as it had been the previous year.

We retraced our steps to all the major cities and towns. Once again, in places such as Birmingham, Liverpool, Manchester, Edinburgh or Glasgow, the fans were there in their hordes and as enthusiastic as before.

Reactions to this crazy show never ceased to amaze me. The show itself had become even sillier with Paul and I constantly digressing from the already flimsy script. I found myself in the role of 'straight feed' to a wonderful comedian or should I say 'comedienne.'

Paul/Lily has one of the sharpest wits I have ever known, let alone worked opposite.

Paul O'Grady as Lily Savage has the most outrageous turns of phrase and lightning fast patter. One can't help but think that this stems from being a 'scouse' a Liverpudlian who grew up with the Irishness of his family and especially the presence of a couple of vibrant, eccentric aunts who provided great fuel for his wit.

At times I felt as though I were learning a whole new skill as I tried to keep up with him. Joan Ferguson had now become somewhat of a 'panto villain' and I *loved it*! After all those episodes of sour faces and tough actions, goofing around and taking the piss out of her was heaven.

Previously, there had been a newspaper poll taken in the UK to find out who was considered the greatest screen villain. Among the 'baddies' of the eighties were Larry Hagman as J.R. Ewing in *Dallas* and of course Joan Collins as Alexis in *Dynasty*. There I was, listed among the most dastardly demons of the small screen. Lo and behold, I, a.k.a. Joan Ferguson, won the poll hands down – a rather dubious honour and not one that I had envisaged for myself all those years ago in the John Alden Shakespeare Company, but I was quietly chuffed at the result.

Of course, television is all-powerful in the homes of people everywhere and none more so perhaps in countries like Britain where inclement weather and very short winter days keeps so many people indoors. It is extraordinary that the popularity of *Prisoner* and its characters is so strong after forty years. The fans are incredibly knowledgeable about the episodes, the characters and the actors who played them. I sometimes wonder where my career as a jobbing actor would have taken me without the intense exposure of *Prisoner*.

Never in my wildest dreams did I expect to acquire the fan base that I seem to have.

Such is the power of television!

The fact that we are in people's living rooms every week produces a very different kind of fan to those who go to the theatre occasionally. People who go to the theatre actively seek out productions and leave the comfort of their living rooms. I have noted over the years (with delight!) that many people who have followed a television character or actor make the effort to see that actor in a stage show. I know of a number of fans who had never been to the theatre before watching *Prisoner* who have since become avid theatre goers. As many television actors cross over into film and theatre this is a good thing for the survival of live performance.

Fandom is a curious beast and fans come in many shapes and sizes. They can be shy, and they can be pushy. They can be rude or even be downright creepy. Sometimes I get the feeling that it takes some courage to approach us, I see this hesitancy in their demeanour and I find their shyness charming. Most are extremely polite and it's great to chat with them. Some are very demanding and get quite miffed if they are passed over for another fan. Generally, I have noticed that many of the fans have actually become friends through following actors' careers. I'm not aware of any romances that have blossomed among them, but, you never know!

The advent of social media has opened a Pandora's box of fandom and although I don't subscribe to any of those intrusive sites I am aware of the communication between followers of television shows. Sometimes there seems to be a cult of 'one upmanship' among them regarding who knows what about certain shows and actors.

The truth of the matter is that they don't know *us*.

Sometimes, I get the feeling that they are unable to distinguish the actor from the character. I have been aware over the years that some people haven't been able to separate me from Joan Ferguson. Naturally, these are people who have not met me.

Over the years I have met some terrific people here and overseas. I am always delighted to see them. I have met kind, generous and caring people who have loyally followed my career since 1982. It has given me great pleasure to meet these people at the stage door of a theatre when I have finished a performance or to chat with them at events organised for us all to get together.

Many of these fans have been extremely generous with gifts and their time. I have received flowers, hand-made trinkets, Waterford crystal, Korean artefacts, paintings and sketches (some horrendous but still very well meant), bottles of Scotch and wine and I have even had a star named after me by a fan in England. All of which I have appreciated greatly.

Sometimes though, I will admit, I have been less than gracious to the fans. For instance, when approaching the stage door in readiness for a performance I am often annoyed to find a group of fans waiting. In England this really bugged me. Prior to a performance is *no time* to approach an actor wanting autographs, photos or a chat. Afterwards by all means! It is always a pleasure to chat after but never before, when the actor's mind is on other things. The time to sparkle is *after* the show!

I have already mentioned dear Robert Cope in the UK. He came into my life back in 1991 with a fan letter and has been there ever since. His first letter to 'Miss Kirkpatrick' is now Dear Mags or Hey, old girl. Barry Campbell in Scotland I also regard as a dear friend more than a fan and his ability to organise an event is fantastic.

In the light of the way my acting career actually turned out, I sometimes muse over the early dreams I had of playing the great Shakespearian roles and of the ambition I once had to record Shakespeare's sonnets and the Australian poetry that I so loved.

But these musings are few and far between.

I have never thought much about this 'fame' thing. I have always considered myself to be simply a 'jobbing actor'.

If what I have experienced since *Prisoner* is 'FAME' then so be it. I am very uncomfortable with the current trend to use such words as 'Icon', 'Legend', 'Star' and other such hyperbolic terms in relation to the current crop of mediocrity. It seems that these descriptions are over-used today in relation to participants involved in reality TV – in my opinion often a pathetic group of would be 'stars' seeking their fifteen minutes of fame.

As far as other actors are concerned, if their body of work warrants it then I am happy for whatever fame comes their way. In recent times we have seen the rise of extremely talented Australian actors taking their place among the world's best and that makes me very proud.

As for me, I'm a jobbing actor. It's my *job*.

The pragmatist in me wins every time, but if that pragmatism takes me to places I would never have imagined, I'm not complaining.

It is what it is.

CHAPTER TEN

TRAVELS THROUGH
THE COUNTRY

Home once again, and after a period of settling into home life again I was off on another adventure on the other side of the country.

4000 kms away in Perth, Western Australia, was the Perth Playhouse, and its artistic director, Alan Becher, offered me a role. Alan, who had been a successful actor himself was a friend from my old New Theatre days. The play was Kay Mellor's, *A Passionate Woman*. The character, Betty was an unhappy Leeds housewife, a doting mother who finds the thought of her beloved son leaving home to marry too much to bear. She retreats to the attic and among the memorabilia of her youth, she relives the passionate affair she had before getting bogged down in her listless marriage. And that marriage leads her to rebelling and she spends most of Act 2 on her rooftop. Defiantly refusing to come down despite the pleas of her husband and son. Eventually, the husband astonishes her by arriving in a hot air balloon and persuading her to get on board. This, she does and they drift off into the sunset, proving that deep down, her stodgy husband really did have a romantic streak. It was a dream of a role and I was working with a cast of fine actors, who, along with Alan guiding us, made this a most enjoyable experience.

My greatest challenge was the Leeds accent. Imagine my relief and delight when on opening night the chairman of the theatre board asked Alan what part of Yorkshire I was from!

As WA has an enormous number of immigrants from the British Isles, it was not inconceivable that I could be the genuine article. My next confidence boost came from a group of women leaving the theatre after a matinee. On meeting me, one of them enthusiastically gushed in a broad Yorkshire accent, 'Ee, you were joost like me'. Well, I was as pleased as punch. Great praise indeed. Irish, Upper class English, Dutch, American, broad Australian, even Central European accents had been pretty good, if I say so myself, but a regional, northern accent I had never attempted.

Maybe by some strange means I had ingested something of those regions on various trips to the North.

When the season was over, I embarked on another adventure. I was going to drive those 4000 kms across the Nullarbor.

I had mentioned the plan to my old friend Paul Jones and he thought it a splendid idea and said he would love to be a part of it.

Paul is probably my oldest friend from our teenage years in Newcastle. He was part of the great Aussie exodus to London in the early sixties and had lived there ever since. So it was agreed and Paul flew out from England to Perth. The only catch was that Paul didn't drive, so there would be no relief driver for me but at least I would have someone to talk to.

We set off on December 1 carrying in our camper van along with luggage a good supply of coffee, coffee pot, good wine glasses (I hate to drink out of cheap glasses), insect repellent, games of Scrabble, Yahtzee and a deck of cards – not quite 'grey nomads' but near enough.

We bypassed Fremantle and motored on to Mandurah where we stocked up on the necessary supplies. Then on through Pinjarra, Harvey, Bunbury to Busseltown, a pleasant town with the longest jetty in the Southern Hemisphere (2 kilometres – over a mile) – then along the coast of Geographe Bay to Canal Rocks, a beautiful setting of campers, cottages and villas. We made ourselves comfortable then settled down to watch the sunset sipping a very pleasant chilled rosé. We had a simple first meal on the road of ham, cheese, crusty bread and tomatoes drizzled with olive oil. We had a rousing game of Scrabble and chatted to two charming young travellers on a surfing safari. I got up at one point through the night to go to the toilet and almost collided with a kangaroo. I'm not sure who got the bigger shock, but it frightened the daylights out of me and made my run for the loo even faster.

The next morning, we had a brisk walk around the foreshore and up the rocks to higher ground to admire the view. The air was so refreshing. On the way up, we met a pair of kangaroos who gave us a brief staring competition before they bounded away.

Time to hit the road again. I had decided to drive for eight hours each day with appropriate rest stops for food or sightseeing. It was advisable not to drive at dusk and I certainly wasn't going to drive at night, so come 5 pm each day it was time to switch off the engine, unload for our meal and open a cold bottle, sit back and enjoy the sunset.

Our next stop was to visit the Mammoth Cave, a huge limestone cave with massive stalactites and stalagmites and fossils. There were a series of caves almost like different rooms, each one more breathtaking. They were both majestic and eerie. An unforgettable experience.

Then it was on to Cape Leewin and the lighthouse. This is the most south western point of the continent and is where the Indian and Great Southern Oceans meet. The view from the lighthouse gives a vague idea of the enormity and danger of these great oceans.

After the bracing air of Cape Leewin it was on to the great Karri forests of Pemberton, Walpole, Denmark and Nornalup (which means 'place of black snake').

We went on the Eco Tour in the forest to end all forests. The tree top walk was the most wonderful experience, to walk among these giant trees and to reach out and touch them almost to the top was thrilling beyond belief. Then there was the Giant Tingle tree, a hollowed out giant in which 100 people could fit. Its height was more than 30 m (98 feet) and the circumference at breast height 22.3 m (73 feet).

The south-western region of Australia is hard to leave, and we spent far more time there than intended and we didn't even get to the world-famous

Margaret River wine region. Words such as awe inspiring, majestic and magical hardly do justice to the sights we had seen.

Our next stop was Albany, the oldest colonial settlement in WA. It had been founded as a military outpost of NSW in 1826 as part of a plan to forestall French ambitions in the area. During the last decade of the 19th century the town served as the gateway to the Eastern Goldfields. For many years it was the colony's only deep-water port and then was the last port of call for troop ships departing Australia in the First World War and thus is connected to the legend of ANZAC.

We then travelled on through Mallee scrub and wheat belt country past Jerramungup, Ravensthorpe and Hopetoun where we set up for the night in a caravan park by the ocean. The weather had turned, and the wild stormy winds coming off the Great Southern Ocean forced us to take refuge in one of the rather tacky caravans, but at least we were dry.

The next morning it was on to Esperance and north to Norseman and then due east to Balladonia.

We were then on a road that goes for 145 kms (96 miles) without a curve or bend of any description. Despite the grey skies and occasional rain, the country side was spectacular, low scrub with some late flowering wildflowers, extraordinary bird life, daring emus crossing the highway, kangaroos drinking rainwater at the edge of the road – all giving us a cursory glance and then going about their business.

One of the most intriguing sights was approaching a wedge-tail eagle feasting on road kill. As he was evident from a distance along this straight road, I was able to slow down and give some blasts on the horn. Eventually, I stopped altogether and watched in amazement as this wondrous creature ever so slowly lifted his vast wings and moved to a dead tree on the roadside, then resumed his feasting when we had passed.

We were on the road to the comically named Cocklebiddy. The weather had turned really nasty and the rain was lashing down and the wind made driving the higher than normal vehicle a touch difficult. So we stopped at the aptly named Wedgetail Inn. This was a typical 'truckie's stop' complete with bar, cafe, pool table, juke box, motel accommodation and naturally, the usual 'colourful' characters.

We had certainly picked a good night to stay and the next day was the arrival of the supply truck and that meant that locals from far away were in to get their supplies the next day and of course to make the outing complete, have a good time.

We had a hoot of a time with a bunch of really good, down to earth people of this remote area.

Taking off the next morning after a big country breakfast, we continued to strike rotten weather. The irony of having rain follow me across this driest of lands did not escape me.

Occasionally, we would stop and look down from the cliff tops into the Great Australian Bight in the hope that a whale or seal might be passing by. It was in vain that we risked life and limb on those windswept cliff tops.

Then through Madura, Mundrabilla, Eucla and then finally over the border into South Australia.

On then to Ceduna and Streaky Bay on the western side of the Eyre peninsula. We were now moving into a region world famous for its seafood – oysters, crayfish, whiting and tuna, not to forget the prized abalone. The whiting at Streaky Bay didn't disappoint. It was then on to Coffin Bay in search of the famous oysters.

This area brought back a delicious memory of once touring South Australia in the play, *The One Day of the Year*.

We had done a Saturday night performance in Port Lincoln and the next day, Sunday, was our day off. A barbecue was arranged for us by some of the charming locals. During the fun of the day, I found myself attracted to a very handsome, out-doorsy type of man. The feeling was obviously mutual, and we were getting along famously when he suggested that we go and get some crayfish. Instructions were left with our hosts to put the fire on and get the water boiling. Armed with a chilled bottle of wine for the trip, we took off on a bumpy ride across scrubland and dirt roads to a deserted beach on the other side of the Peninsula. There was a tiny boat on the sand and we rowed out to a trawler at anchor in the bay. When on board, he brought up over the side a basket full of gleaming crayfish.

We sat there for some time drinking the wine and marvelling at the sight of the full moon rising in the East and the blood red sun going down over the water in the West, a very romantic setting you might say. Well, *of course* one thing led to another and by the time we got back to the party the pot was well and truly boiling and a bunch of hungry actors was waiting with knowing grins on their faces – a sweet memory.

On this trip, however, there were no crayfish to be had but the delicious Coffin Bay oysters did just as well. The bird life, sparkling ocean and sweeping sandy beaches make this peninsula just one of myriad breathtaking places in this country.

From there to Port Lincoln, extremely flourishing back then with the tuna industry thriving.

Then on up the Spencer Gulf past wheat fields and prosperous homesteads to Whyalla. This vast steel town seemed to have had the life sucked out of it – shops boarded up, empty streets, idle youths hanging around street corners. A real sense of *loss* pervaded the town. Happily, after years of downturn, that is all about to change. As I write, news has come through of foreign investments coming into Whyalla which will breathe new life and prosperity into what was long ago a thriving centre of industry.

Port Augusta was next and then on to the Flinders Ranges. The rain had not diminished the beauty of these ranges, but I would have loved to see them in the bright sunlight as they have been depicted in the wonderful paintings of Hans Heysen.

On through Wilmington and Orroroo to Peterborough and more wheat belt country. We stayed at a typical country pub with typical country food – hearty serves of roast lamb, mint sauce and vegetables, apple pie and custard, enormous breakfasts of eggs, bacon, sausages, mushrooms – the lot! And a typical country landlord, a most pleasant overnight stay.

Then to Broken Hill and a quick look around this frontier mining town.

Silver and lead had been discovered long ago and led to the beginnings of the giant corporation BHP (Broken Hill Propriety).

This city, or its surrounds, gained some notoriety through the book and film *Wake in Fright*. *Wake in Fright*, a novel by Kenneth Cook which takes its name from an old curse, 'May you dream of the Devil and wake in fright'. It is a psychological thriller which tells of the nightmare endured by a young schoolteacher, new to the outback and faced with the madness and violence of drunken locals. It is a vicious tale of dehumanising savagery and it has become a cult classic.

When I was on tour there in 1972, the local theatre folk denied that there was any similarity with their city. However, the local identities in the bar of the pub where we were staying emphatically agreed that 'The Hill' was just like that as shown in the film. We certainly didn't see any of the brutality as depicted in the film, but we took their word for it. After all, the myth lent a certain rakish charm to this wild west town.

After Broken Hill we headed for Cobar and were then on the way home, more or less.

On this leg of the trip something happened that has haunted me ever since.

In the early morning driving along a deserted highway, I came across a kangaroo, recently hit, no doubt by a truck. The poor creature, still alive, was in the middle of the road, its lower body crushed. What I saw were the beautiful brown eyes of this wonderful creature, his head raised and front paws reaching with almost a pleading look in those great sad eyes.

I was helpless to do anything. I burst into tears and slowly drove around this wretched dying animal. I now know why country folk carry a rifle or a heavy implement. To put that suffering beast out of its horror would be the humane thing to do.

Cobar was a pleasant town and a meal at the local pub was more than adequate. The bartender was an avid theatre goer with lots of stories to tell. One of the local lads turned out to be an old friend of actress Justine Saunders.

Growing up in Australia in the forties and fifties I lived in a suburban, predominately white environment, so my knowledge of the first people of this country was non-existent. In school we were taught about James Cook and Arthur Phillip but only from a British perspective, as indeed was most of the history taught in those days. We were never given any information about the invasion or the massacres or indeed anything at all about the 'stolen generations' – children taken from their parents and raised by the Government or well-meaning white people because their own, real parents weren't, supposedly, 'good enough'.

I wasn't aware of any obvious racism around me, although pejorative terms such as 'Abo' and 'Boong', peppered general white conversation when referring to anyone of darker skin. The only aborigines that I was aware of as a child were Harold Blair, the great singer, Pastor Doug Nichols – elite sportsman, man of religion and a pioneer for reconciliation – and Dave Sands – world champion boxer, inducted into the American Boxing Hall of Fame who was lauded in our house because he came from the region, more so than for the colour of his skin.

It wasn't until the early seventies that I actually *spoke* to an indigenous person, I'm ashamed to say.

Living nearby in Balmain was a woman named Heather Pitt who was a noted singer. Heather had been part of a group, with her two sisters Sophie and Georgia, called *The Harmony Sisters* and they had performed extensively throughout World War 2 entertaining the troops.

Heather was from Cairns, in Far North Queensland, and originally from the Torres Strait Islands.

She was elegant and gracious, and I enjoyed many neighbourly chats with her.

A lasting memory of Heather is of her standing at a bus stop, chatting with me as she waited to go to a singing gig. As we gossiped away, Caitlin, who was probably three at the time was silently stroking Heather's manicured, bejewelled and very dark hand. I felt slightly apprehensive, wondering what was going to come next. Fears were totally dispelled when Caitlin piped up 'Heather, you've got beautiful hands.'

Out of the mouths of babes, truth without filter!

It was a couple of years later that I encountered the great Bob Maza. I was playing in Chekhov's *The Seagull*, which I have previously mentioned was directed by Brian Syron. After returning from New York, Brian was easing himself into the dual world of white establishment theatre and the burgeoning Aboriginal Theatre. He introduced me to Bob and over supper we spoke of Chekhov, Shakespeare and Bob's dreams of a National Aboriginal Theatre. I don't know what I expected from him, but I was in awe of this imposing, erudite man whose passion for the future of his people and the arts was palpable. I am privileged to have known him.

To this day, indigenous actors, writers directors, film makers and dancers are cutting a welcome swathe through the cultural world. Pioneers such as Bob, Jack Charles and Justine Saunders paved the way for the contribution now being made by some remarkable talents.

Justine often referred to herself as a 'little black duck'. Justine was from the Kanomie clan on Great Keppel Island in Queensland. She featured in film, television and theatre *long* before any of her other indigenous sisters came to prominence. Long before diversity in casting became the norm, Justine had broken through whatever barriers had been in place. She was a pioneer who paved the way for the wonderful array of talented women who now grace our screens and stages, who direct our films and write our scripts. In many cases these actors are now cast for their talent and not for the colour of their skin.

In fact, her role as a psychologist in *Prisoner* made *no* reference whatsoever to her ethnicity. It was a first back then. Sadly, Justine died in 2007, just as the great resurgence of indigenous culture was taking a firm footing in the arts scene of this country.

How proud 'Aunty' Justine would be that her pioneering ultimately bore such sweet fruit.

* * *

Next morning began the last leg of the trip home. Eight or nine hours away.

My cross-continent adventure had taken ten fabulous days. I had seen sights that took my breath away, met people who embodied the spirit of all that is good in this country. By the time I arrived back at South Maroota and home I had travelled 5251 kms and the journey confirmed through and through, despite some poor weather, that I am blessed to live in a remarkable country.

Actors are everywhere and people are naturally curious about them. I understand this. Actors are just people but the demands of the work call us to use all our experiences to inform our roles. That's why actors need experiences – to provide the raw material from which we draw.

Much has been written and taught about the art of acting. Greater minds and talents than I have expounded their theories and methods to generations of aspiring thespians. To try and absorb all that advice would leave one's head spinning and cause utter conflict when approaching a role.

I have nothing profound or new to offer, I simply know what I know, from the sum total of all my experiences.

Like many before me I read Stanislavsky's *An Actor Prepares*. It was revolutionary in its day. Prior to Stanislavsky the profession was dominated by 'declamatory acting' a style where actors would say their lines as if they were making speeches, complete with exaggerated gestures and even more exaggerated facial expressions. After Stanislavsky, actors strove for a more natural interpretation of their roles. I found it to be an exercise in common sense. Stanislavsky's 'method' was not the earth-shattering breakthrough I had naively expected. But, nevertheless, to me it laid the groundwork for truthful performances. I found nothing high-falutin' or esoteric – just wisdom and insight.

Actors have different ways of approaching a role. In contrast to the 'fly by the seat of your pants' reality of the day-to-day workings of TV series acting, theatre is vastly different.

For starters, there is much more time for preparation.

First comes the audition, for which an actor should have done at least some cursory research into the play. The actor needs to understand the playwright, the style of the piece and whether it is contemporary or classic.

Then when rehearsals begin the search continues into the character, the time, the place – anything that gives the actor a deeper understanding of the role.

Often a rehearsal room will display all manner of pertinent references including pictures of the period, costumes, newspaper clippings and set designs.

Discussions will take place between actors and the director and often these can be quite robust and opinionated as artistic decisions about interpretations are made.

Ultimately it is up to the actor to do their homework. They have to research the character they are playing, delve into the characters' back stories and discover the essence of the characters – their personalities and how those personalities 'show up' – the body language, the accents, the mannerisms. We *have to* draw on the all the observations that have accumulated over the years. We need to decide where the character comes from, their intentions and their reasons for being where they are.

In many cases this sort of information is evident in the writing of the play. If not, then information regarding locations and lifestyles is readily available in a reference library, or should I say nowadays Google and Wikipedia too?

Once I was given a role that gave me no background information other than 'working class Mum' I certainly knew what that was about, but in order to fully develop the character and my performance, I wrote a detailed life picture as I saw her. In doing this I managed to become deeply embedded in the truth of the character. The actor playing my husband, the wonderful Ron Graham, claimed that he found my back story beneficial to his own performance too.

In David Williamson's play *Emerald City*, the character of Elaine was presented to me with one description, 'a literary agent'. No light was shed on any other characteristic. Once again, I invented a history for this very different character. It was possibly loosely based on my then perception of women in positions of power in the film and literary world as there were a number of strong women in those positions at the time. I think I took a little of each of them and added a spot of me. It served me well and rounded out my performance.

'Know who you are' is a mantra for any actor along with the usual thoughts of 'Why am I here?', 'What do I want to achieve from this scene?' and 'What is my attitude to such-and- such a character?'.

It's all very basic. There's no 'magic' involved. Intuition has always played a big part in my work and many times when I have doubted myself, directors have told me to trust my instincts.

Trusting my instincts invariably works.

I think I can safely say that I am much more instinctive than intellectual as an actor.

Sometimes a difficult role comes along, or a character difficult to understand, or even *like*. Many years ago, when cast as a person who represented everything I loathe in terms of giggly, vacuous females, in order to overcome my awkwardness and distaste for the character, the late Max Phipps gave me some very sage advice.

'Expose her!' he said.

Pretty good advice I thought, and extremely helpful in playing someone the polar opposite of me. But it's also good advice to expose yourself too.

So when you see an actor shedding tears and wondering, 'How does she do that on cue?' bear in mind that the actor might be thinking about a beautiful sunset, or a moment of regret, or perhaps even a dying kangaroo on a road she couldn't save.

Me at four

Dad.

Me as a toddler.

With Chrissie, around 1950.

With mum, approximately three years old.

At Newcastle Legacy. Governor General, Sir William Slim. Possibly 1953.

About 4 years old.

Pregnant, with my
mother Chrissie on
Newcastle Beach, 1965.

With Norman Kirkpatrick, 1965.

With Norman and Caitlin in Balmain, around 1970.

My first real Aussie role. *We Find a Bunyip*.

Irene 1973-4.

With Noni Hazelhurst *Don't Piddle Against the Wind*.

With Susannah York. *Shoehorn Sonata.*
Kings Head Theatre, London March 1996.

With Monica Maughan and Kevin
Palmer. *Farewell Brisbane Ladies.*
[Photo: David Wilson 1981]

The One Day of the Year Tom Burlinson, Peter Cummins, Bill Austin
[Photo: David Wilson]

Irene with Noel Ferrier. He finally succeeded in making me laugh!

With Robyn Nevin. *Ham Funeral*
1989. Sydney Theatre Co.

With Ray Meagher. *The Cassidy Album:*
Furtive Love.

The last shot.

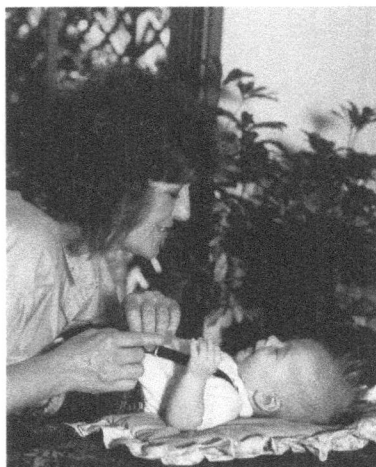

New grandmother. With baby
Daniel early 1990.

My granddaughter, Megan.

A new great grandmother,
with Amelia.

At my grandson's wedding
with Daniel and Brittany.

Four generations. With Chrissie, Megan and Caitlin.

Breakfast with an orang-utan. Singapore 2002.

With Craig Bennett at The
Friar's Club in New York City.

With Maria Venturi, Paula Duncan
and Carlotta.

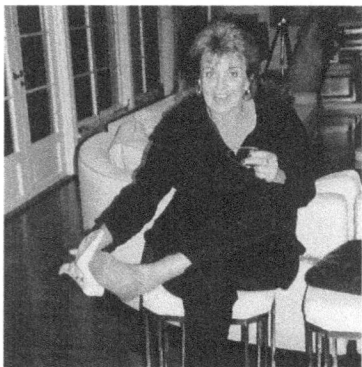

Trying on Marilyn Monroe's
shoe from *The Seven Year Itch*.

With Julie Anthony. *Irene*.

Eating ice cream with Helen
Reddy and Craig Bennett in
Malibu.

With Kevin Palmer, 1986.

With John Tasker.

With Sammy Davis Jnr. Las Vegas,
January 1986

With Bill Cosby.

With Craig
Bennett,
Anne
Phelan
and Craig
Murchie.

With Rod Taylor (Ginger and
Daddy-o) *Welcome to Woop Woop.*

With award-winning make-up artist
Cassie Hanlon, after I shaved my
head. *Welcome to Woop Woop.*

With Paul Bertram on Clark Island.
Children's show *Pirates at the Barn.*

2 Ugly Sisters. With Carlotta in
Cinderella.

With Joy Westmore, Anne Phelan, Val Lehman, Jane Clifton, Betty Bobbitt, Elspeth Ballantyne, Patsy King, Carol Burns. *Behind the Bars: The Prisoner Cell Block H Companion.*

With Lily Savage (Paul O'Grady) *Prisoner Cell Block H The Musical.* Queen's Theatre London, 1985.

With Paul O'Grady, a.k.a Lily Savage. London West End. Opening night *Prisoner Cell Block H* .

As Madame Morrible in *Wicked*. [Photos: Jeff Busby]

CHAPTER ELEVEN

REST AND RESTORATION

What a dream run I'd had since 1995! Two productions of *Shoehorn Sonata*, a West End season, two national tours of the UK, a movie and a successful cabaret show.

Of course, these sorts of highs don't come all the time in this business. Indeed, I had my share of 'resting' or 'considering scripts' as unemployment is euphemistically known in the acting world. In fact, it is that period in an actor's life when you are simply not wanted.

The old rejection game again.

Naturally, to keep body and soul together, we must do other things. Wait tables, sell shoes, pull beers or go on the dole. Not being skilled in any other areas, these were the options open to me. But registering for unemployment benefits is not only soul-destroying but fraught with bureaucratic gobbledygook as to make one not want to go through with the procedure. Years of experience in the performing arts was a skill that seemed to escape the mindset of the person responsible for approving the fortnightly pittance. Making a person feel as though they were a burden on society seemed to be part of the training process in the public service.

So, the rounds began again. The interviews, the auditions, the 'cattle calls', and with each rejection my confidence waned.

This was the case when I was invited to audition for the Sydney Theatre Company's production of Edward Albee's *A Delicate Balance*. I accepted the invitation and dutifully studied the script. *A Delicate Balance* is a drama about the uneasy existence of an upper middle class American family. Agnes, husband

Tobias and Agnes' alcoholic sister Claire, have their lives disrupted by the arrival of old friends Harry and Edna, empty nesters who have come to stay seeking escape from some unnamed terror. Into this mix comes Agnes and Tobias' daughter Julia, seeking refuge after the collapse of her fourth marriage. It is a totally dysfunctional household, a scenario that Albee was so brilliant at creating, *Who's Afraid of Virginia Wolfe* being his best-known masterpiece.

The role of Claire is a beauty and I really wanted to play her – challenging but wonderful to play. A functioning alcoholic, glamourous, sardonic and at times very funny, but with a good amount of pathos thrown in as we witness the decline of the relationship with her sister and the demise of the lives around them.

Simon Phillips was to direct, and with a fear I had never known I took myself off to the audition. The pain got worse as I watched some of our finest actors come and go out of that audition and my confidence plummeted and the urge to flee was very strong.

However, sense prevailed, and I stayed. I had taken some considerable time studying the play and the scene I was to read. Sometimes, on reading a script, the essence of the character leaps out at you and you feel at one with it. Happily, this had been the case on a number of occasions in my career. Maxine in *Night of the Iguana*, Bridie in *Shoehorn Sonata*, and Aggie in *A Hard God* to name a few.

This time it was Claire who leapt off the page to me. It was evident that she was an alcoholic and given *my own* fragile state at the time, I empathised. The alcohol-induced meltdowns, the unacceptable behaviour and melancholy guilt all stood me in good stead at that time in my complete understanding of the character.

I must have been on the money because Simon cast me, and I even went on to win an award – the Variety Club of Australia award for best performance in a play.

Simon Phillips is a wonderful director, a funny, quirky and warm-hearted person. I have enormous regard for him. Sadly, this was to be my only production with him.

The cast was dazzling! Michael Craig; Dinah Shearing, whom I had long admired since the golden years of radio drama in the fifties; Jane Harders and the late Don Reid with whom I had worked in *The Ripper Show* back in the seventies; and dear Heather Mitchell. Heather and I had previously worked together in *Blood Relations*, so it was a joy to be playing her aunt in this complex family saga. Heather was pregnant at the time and suffering terribly in that first trimester. However, she bravely forged on and the ever-attentive stage management thoughtfully placed receptacles in the wings for her emergency dash off stage to throw up.

It was a privilege to work with such a stellar cast, crew and director and some of the old confidence in my ability was restored, even though I was terrible at yodelling and playing the piano accordion, both of which were faked unmercifully. Such a ham!

Breaking the ice with the Sydney Theatre Company then saw a happy relationship develop. Next, in October of that year, came Martin McDonagh's *The Cripple of Inishmaan*. In true McDonagh style, this is a dark, macabre yet funny play. His works are known for their brutal edge yet outrageously funny moments. His screenplay and direction of the film *Three Billboards Outside Ebbing, Missouri* won great acclaim and many awards.

Set on an island off the coast of Galway in Ireland it tells the story of Billy, a handicapped boy who desperately wants to leave the island. He is known to all as 'Cripple Billy' as if it were his given name and he is a target for torment by the hard-hearted locals. When a film crew come to town, Billy decides that he has to get away and become a 'fillum' star. It is a dark comedy filled with eccentric characters all trying to thwart Billy's dreams.

Delving deep into the ways of the people from the remote Aran island, *Inishmaan* was made all the more stimulating by having Maeliosa Stafford directing us. His knowledge of the people of Galway made our research all the more exciting. There was such attention to detail from him that we began to feel as though we actually came from the rugged west of Ireland.

Playing one of the spinster sisters opposite Annie Byron gave me a whole new perspective on the use of *stillness* on stage. I had certainly mastered that on camera during *Prisoner* but the tendency to fidget on stage is a common one. I felt that my character would fuss over her little shop, but that was not to be. Maeliosa assured me that in the boredom of her existence in this God forsaken place, any extra activity would be unheard of. So, I spent a great deal of the play leaning on the shop counter, staring into space only moving or speaking as required and then in a most desultory manner. This felt strange during rehearsals but proved to be most effective. The season was very successful, and I had the pleasure of working with wonderful people. Among them were young actors, Essie Davis, Damon Herriman and Dan Spielman, all of whom have gone on to successful, international careers. Their talents were very evident then and it was no surprise that success came their way.

In May of 1999 I was called into the theatre when an emergency had occurred. Ruth Cracknell had taken ill. She was appearing in a production of *She Stoops to Conquer* opposite the great Leo McKern of *Rumpole of the Bailey* fame. Leo had gone to the UK in 1946 and had carved out an amazing career on the British stage and in such films as *Ryan's Daughter*, and *A Man for all Seasons*. He had won a Best Actor award for his role in the Australian film *Travelling North*.

For my sins, I was to go on 'with the book' that is I would be reading the part, while taking part in the action. The season had been booked out, obviously because of Leo's star power, and the season was limited so there was no chance of cancelling for one night.

So, I was squeezed into a costume, given a quick read through and a rudimentary run of the moves and then I was ON.

I have no idea what sort of person becomes an actor. Popular opinions range from being shy and introverted to being loud and extroverted. We aren't much different to any other profession. It takes all types. But whatever sort of person you are, as an actor, sometimes, life's experiences can translate into performance.

Along with researching a character and what makes them tick, life's experiences can give an insight and bring a depth to a portrayal that might otherwise be lacking. Essentially, I believe that an actor's best tool is the power of observation. Taking in those around him or her, their mannerisms, foibles and little differences. I have always been an inquisitive person and was often chided as child for staring at people and listening in. Sometimes a role can be painful to express honestly but this is often overcome by rehearsing and getting rid of unwanted emotions during that process and thus finding a way to truthfully present the situation without having a nervous breakdown every night.

As nerve wracking as it was, all was going as well as could be expected until a moment when Leo, on stage, was giving forth. I was absolutely transfixed by his performance, so much so that I was oblivious of the stares from my fellow actors, until a nudge in the ribs brought me back to the book in my hand and the words I was to utter. Lesson learned – get your hero worship out of the way during rehearsals!

In July of 1999 came another offer from the STC. It was another McDonagh play, *The Beauty Queen of Leenane*. I had seen this play as part of a trilogy performed by the renowned Druid Theatre Company from Galway in Ireland. It was an experience never to be forgotten as all three plays were performed in the one day.

To sit through three productions is a marathon for audience and actors alike but an extremely exhilarating one. I had experienced this before with *Nicholas Nickleby* and performing in Peter Kenna's trilogy, *The Cassidy Album*. To know that the audience has been with you all day is a joy.

This latest production of *Beauty Queen* was to be directed by Garry Hynes, one of the co-founders of The Druid Company. I was cast as Mag Folan, the selfish, cantankerous, demanding mother of Maureen, the 'Beauty Queen' – the basis of the play being that old Mag Folan constantly stops any success at happiness for her spinster daughter, Maureen.

Having seen Mag played by Marie Mullen, also one of the founders of Druid, I approached the role with great caution.

My fears were dispelled by the presence of the cast. Pamela Rabe as Maureen, Darren Weller and Greg Stone as Pato and Ray. Along with Garry's superb direction, I once again delved into the dark brutal world of McDonagh's writing.

To share the stage with these three remarkable actors reminded me of the old saying that acting is a team effort. The parry and thrust of the dialogue and the action, to me, is akin to a top-level tennis match where players are only as good as those around them.

A successful opening in Sydney was made all the sweeter for me by a comment made by the late Ruth Cracknell, much admired doyenne of theatre, film and television. As I came out of the dressing room on opening night, I was greeted by Ruth and after some very kind words of congratulations, she said, 'I could almost smell that woman.' High praise indeed, I thought because Mag Folan was a sedentary, grubby, unhygienic character. I knew exactly what Ruth meant and I was delighted.

Through the winter of that year we took the play to Melbourne, Brisbane Adelaide and a country tour throughout NSW and Victoria with great success.

Margaret 'Peggy' Ramsay was an Australian-born play agent in London. Probably the most influential playwright's agent in the second half of the twentieth century. Among her famous clients were Joe Orton, Robert Bolt, Alan Ayckbourn, Caryl Churchill and Alan Plater, who wrote the play *Peggy for You,* a title taken from words spoken by her secretary when making calls to clients. John Krummel, artistic director of the Marian Street Theatre, was to produce this play and invited me to play Peggy.

The play takes place in the office of Peggy's agency. She is visited by three playwright clients. An older writer who challenges her authority, a successful dramatist tainted by success and a raw beginner full of ideals, ideas and ambition. She deals with each of them and their problems in her inimitable fashion, revealing along the way her toughness and her vulnerability. One can only presume that the three writers are based on real playwrights with perhaps the young one a vague representation of the late Joe Orton, a highly controversial and ground-breaking figure. One of Peggy's many aphorisms was, 'Drama, like sex, should never be rushed.'

Aside from the fact that I was not an agent, some minor similarities popped up.

1) Ramsay was born in Molong NSW – a small country town well known

to me due to the fact that a favourite uncle lived there, and I often visited.

2) Her nickname was Peggy, as indeed was mine for the first three years of my life.

3) Perhaps her flamboyance and outspokenness was something that, rightly or wrongly, John perceived in me.

Whatever the reason, I was delighted to accept his offer and with great support on stage from actors of the calibre of David Downer, Michelle Doake, Mark Kilmurry and Amos Szeps, we created a fun successful season. To my surprise and delight, I received a Mo Award for my performance.

It was extremely gratifying to encounter writers and agents who had had dealings with Peggy. They maintained that I had absolutely captured the essence of the woman. What a compliment, I thought, given that I had never met the woman. It must have been Alan Plater's writing. A good writer will show an actor the way every time.

Singin' in the Rain was a lavish stage production based on the all-time favourite film of the same name. In 2000, this new production was being staged around the world. David Atkins was producing it to tour Australia, Hong Kong and Singapore. What an opportunity! To be part of one of my all-time-favourite shows and to see parts of South East Asia totally unfamiliar to me.

David assembled a terrific cast consisting of Todd McKenney, Rachael Beck, the amazing talents of Wayne Scott Kermond, Jackie Love, Vic Rooney, David Goddard and the very funny Glenn Butcher. I was cast as Dora Bailey and the dialect coach engaged to coach Lina Lamont to 'round her vowels'.

The ensemble of dancers, singers and actors was dazzling. The ensemble included the beautiful Sheree de Costa who gave an incredible performance in the iconic segment *Broadway Melody* recreating the role made famous by the great Cyd Charisse in the 1952 film.

Wayne Scott Kermond, third generation entertainer, was a riot performing *Make 'em Laugh* – a tour-de-force that would have had its originator, Donald O' Connor green with envy.

Todd McKenney's *Singin' in the Rain* segment was as exciting on stage as it had been on film all those years ago, when done by Gene Kelly.

We opened in Sydney in May 2001 and moved to Melbourne in September. Brisbane, Adelaide and Perth followed.

In 2002, the Hong Kong/Singapore adventure began. Hong Kong was all the excitement that I had anticipated. We played in a vast Arts Complex to packed houses. It has become evident to me since that the people of South East Asia really go for American musicals in a big way. It was the same later with *Wicked* in Seoul, Singapore and Manila.

Away from the theatre, the delights of Hong Kong consisted mainly of tram, train, bus and ferry travel, all of which I found to be extraordinarily efficient, clean and frequent. Trips across the harbour to Kowloon were a must as was high tea at the famous Peninsula Hotel, such an icon from the Colonial days. The markets were exotic places of retail therapy. The markets and Jardine's Bazaar in Stanley were just a bus ride to experience amazing shopping. A bus ride to the giant Tian Tian Buddha at the Po Lin Monastery was a great adventure. A climb of 268 steps to the Giant Buddha and the museum was an experience not forgotten. The Buddha, a massive bronze statue completed in 1992 on the island of Lantau, stands 43 metres high atop a lotus throne.

So pleased that I was somewhat younger and fitter then. It would be impossible to try now. Although I believe there is now a cable car to the top. Lunch in the restaurant was a vegetarian's dream. Fresh produce farmed on site and lovingly prepared by the monks.

Taking the Peak tram to the top of Victoria Peak was another adventure of the near perpendicular kind. 552 metres up with stops along the way for more shops and then a breathtaking view across to Kowloon and mountains beyond.

While I was in Hong Kong, on October 12, the terrorist bombing in the night club area of Kuta on the island of Bali took place. 202 people were killed, including 88 Australians. The bars and night clubs were crowded with seasonal holiday makers including many Australian sporting teams living it up after a season of competition. Among the fatalities were sports people known to our company manager. An air of sadness and grief descended on the company as we reeled from the shock of lives lost and the sheer brutality of the attack. It somehow made us all feel a little less safe away from home.

When the season ended in Hong Kong, Singapore was to be the next stop. We were given the option of flying home to Australia for the break between countries or going on to Singapore and having ten days of holiday. Naturally, some of us chose the latter and a fun ten days began. Lazing around the pool during the day then off to Raffles for a Singapore Sling. The famous hotel that had seen the likes of so many celebrities since it opened in 1887 was famous for this cocktail. What a disappointment to discover that it now comes out of a dispenser! I had been so looking forward to the theatre of a cocktail maker standing behind the famed Long Bar and flamboyantly serving us.

However, the atmosphere was still rather Noël Coward or Somerset Maugham.

To the hawker food markets for cheap, fantastic food. For the ten days there I think a different cuisine was enjoyed every night. From the Malaysian, the Chinese, Vietnamese, Nonya, Indian and Indonesian. From the chilli crab to the Hainanese chicken rice to the nasi goring, and the laksa to the Hokkein prawn mee and the delights of Arab Street with its Turkish and Mediterranean restaurants. A gourmet paradise for ten blissful days. Such fun we had! Of course, there was more shopping – difficult to avoid when you are in shopping and eating heaven.

Aside from *Prisoner* and *Richmond Hill*, my appearances in some thirty other TV shows have comprised mostly fairly inconsequential roles. Of course, there were two different characters in *Home and Away* and the title role in *Betty's Bunch*, a children's series shot in New Zealand and quality ABC productions such as G.P. and several half-hour comedies.

I did enjoy my first guest role on *All Saints*. A lice-ridden, drunken, foul mouthed bag lady. Of course, the underlying story was the usual cliché – well-educated, privileged, fallen on hard times. Nevertheless, it was great fun to play and I couldn't resist the temptation to improvise the dialogue occasionally.

Along the way there have been theatre and film productions with crazy names – *Snake Gully*; *The Greater Illustrated History of the Glorious Antipodes Show*; *Don't Piddle Against The Wind*; *Mate*; *Up A Gum Tree*; *We Find A Bunyip*; *Childhead's Doll*; *You Know I Can't Hear You When The Water's Running* and of course, *Welcome to Woop Woop*. I'm sure there are others but as I can't remember them then perhaps they are best forgotten anyway.

I have never felt as comfortable in front of the camera as I do on stage. I am always more nervous of an impending TV scene than I am of a stage performance. Except, perhaps, on opening night, but they are the sort of nerves that get me going. The adrenalin, the sense of excitement, of danger, knowing that there is no 'safety' net as in film or TV when one can do another 'take'. The anticipation of that first audience response is thrilling. In comedy, the first laugh is almost like a great weight lifting or the expelling of air after holding the breath for a long time. I never tired of the excitement that theatre brings.

I don't enjoy watching myself on film as I am mostly disappointed. The 'me' in my mind is rarely the 'me' I see on the screen.

The late Bill Hunter once gave me some advice when I had expressed nervousness about a screen role. 'Know who you are,' he said. Well, I have always known who the character I played was, where she came from, background, characteristics, etc. Maybe I just haven't known who *I* was.

As I have previously mentioned I have had the great good fortune to work with some actors whose influences have been profound. Among them is the great Chaim Topol. It was my privilege to play Yente opposite him in a production of *Fiddler on the Roof*. Topol had played Tevye in the film and countless times since, all over the world. His mastery on that stage was awe inspiring. The smallest detail so clearly defined, be it a slight movement of a hand, a turn of the head, a pause, (often very, very long!), I found him to be not only inspirational but a delightful human being, funny, caring and supportive.

I have no other comparisons to make but he is, to me, the definitive Tevye. A theory I am sure is shared by many.

After *Singin' in the Rain*, the next six years included a season of Shaw's *Major Barbara* for the Sydney Theatre Company.

In 2005, I went off to the UK again for another *Prisoner* fan event. This time it was a delightful experience organised by Barry Campbell, a charming young Scot who had formed a company to promote appearances of *Prisoner* alumni, much to the joy of fans.

These events were brilliantly organised, unlike my previous experience in the 90s. Barry and his colleagues, including my friend Rob Cope made every effort to see to the comfort and entertainment of both actors and fans. Every appearance was a delight.

Of course, while in the UK, I naturally had to have time in London. It truly is a remarkable city and I love it. I always make an effort to see London theatre productions. I care only to see what the Brits do best, their own stories. Whether the classics, modern or even the quaintness of JB Priestly and Emlyn Williams. The Broadway musicals on the West End, I give a miss as we do them so well ourselves.

On my return, I was cast as Yente in a season of *Fiddler on the Roof* and it was followed by a national tour of my beloved *Shoehorn Sonata*. Belinda Giblin was with me as Sheila. Bel was wonderful. She is not only a superb actor but a great person. She is funny, clever, extremely erudite and often delightfully bawdy. She is perfect company. As designated driver on our travels, I found her to be not only great company but a dedicated 'lead foot'. She really did enjoy a speedy trip! We had many vigorous discussions about books, politics, art and show business. Our love of cryptic crosswords was a source of friendly rivalry.

Time rolled on as did my life. Nothing exciting happened. I tended my garden, socialised with friends and spent quality time with my family. My grandchildren, Daniel and Megan were growing up fast and as always, the light of my life.

I embarked on a few efforts to be physically fit and, with a moderate degree of success, I took part in aquarobics and signed up to a gym – way out of my comfort zone. All of which at the time of writing have gone out the window except for my early morning swim which is a life-affirming activity.

On the work front, there were a few forays into the world of auditions and screen tests, none of which brought much joy. A bit part in a little movie here, a guest spot on TV there.

As the old show biz saying goes, 'I couldn't get arrested'.

Boy! The eventual irony of that!!!

And, eventually, in 2008, auditions were held for the big new musical *Wicked*. That process required me to do three auditions for the creatives from New York. Finally, Bingo! I was cast as Madame Morrible and thus began seven of the most extraordinary years of my life.

CHAPTER TWELVE

LIFE BECOMES WICKED

M adame Morrible is headmistress of Crage Hall at Shiz University and a cohort of the Wizard. On discovering the amazing powers possessed by Elphaba, the green witch, she sets out to harness those powers for her own evil ambitions.

Wicked was demanding in many ways.

To be a part of this amazing show I was required to relocate to Melbourne for a year. An apartment was found in colourful St. Kilda and so began my new life in wonderful Melbourne. I have always had a soft spot for this most gracious of cities – the ease of getting around, the food, the architecture and cultural delights all so accessible. I have always found the acting fraternity of this city to be close and supportive of each other. When all the theatres in the CBD are in operation, casts and crews from the various productions get together and socialise. Usually on a Thursday (pay day) night after the show. This has become known as Thirsty Thursday and these nights are the source of lots of laughs and urban myths.

Rehearsals for *Wicked* finally began and after the usual 'first day in school' nerves had been eased with coffee, muffins, introductions and reunions, it was down to business.

Six days a week we were cajoled, drilled, encouraged and sometimes bullied a little. All the creatives were from the New York production and at times they had the knack of making us feel that we were less than wonderful, other times they made us feel like winners as they set about re-creating the enormous success of the Broadway production.

Their methods were, to say the least, strenuous. I have always found the American idea of humour rather odd with its absence of irony, but their unfailing politeness, drive and dedication is to be admired.

Eventually, we moved into the theatre for a very long technical rehearsal. The magnificent Regent Theatre is a very grand refurbishment of that bygone time of great theatres, the 1920s.

Front of house is breathtaking in its grandeur but backstage is a nightmare. A rabbit warren of stairs and virtually no space in the wings either side of the stage. The mounting of this enormous production was nothing short of a miracle and a testament to the genius of our backstage crew. That no one was seriously injured is a wonder in itself. In all my years I had never seen a set of such complexity. Entering the auditorium on that first day was like a control room of some vast space project. Every department, electrics, wardrobe, special effects and heaven knows what else was represented in a sea of laptops that lit up the stalls with an eerie green light.

Little by little we found our way around the extraordinary set without injury, thanks to the concise instructions from safety officers.

I had been in this theatre before with *Singin' in the Rain* and I was only too aware of the toll that the multitude of stairs back stage could take on the body. I wasn't prepared for the twelve months of pain and torture as my surroundings and heavy costumes began to take effect on these old bones.

My days off, in the main, were spent in the company of acupuncturist, physiotherapists, osteopaths and rheumatologists. Ah! The glamour of the theatre.

The complex and exciting set was enhanced by the costumes of Susan Hilferty, multi-award-winning designer of stage, film and opera. Her designs were breathtaking in their range and ingenuity, quirky and incredibly innovative, the like of which I had never seen before. Nor had I worn anything quite so heavy.

Costumes are one of my favourite aspects of acting work. I love a good dressing up!

As you can imagine, a costume isn't just a piece of clothing, it's a major element of a performance. Costumes can be expensive to create, they're works of art in themselves and they not only have to look good, they have to be durable. It's important to minimise the risk of damage to a costume and in a theatre production we are often able to work in a facsimile of the costume we will wear. But it's also important that the actor has time to 'live in a costume' so that it is as natural for the actor to wear as it would be for the character that the actor is portraying. For instance, if the play is a period piece then it is essential the actor wears something that resembles the final outfit. Long skirts, corsets and such for the women and maybe breeches and boots for the men. And depending on the play, this could be reversed! Personally, I like to know mainly about the shoes I will be wearing. Sometimes if I get the walk and the stance sorted, then the rest of the costume says it for me. For me, I *literally* have to stand in someone else's shoes to feel that I'm inhabiting a part, and it was particularly important for me to stand in Morrible's shoes, since I was eventually to play her for a much longer time than I had Joan Ferguson.

The challenge not only of the role, but of the make-up and costumes and the sheer physical demands were to be my ongoing dilemma for seven years! The makeup and wig designs had all been executed by the original designers from NYC and for the next seven years were overseen and maintained by Kellie Ritchie, a genius in her own right. The production weeks were fraught with technical and performance problems as the enormity of this project dawned on us all.

Of course, all the drama was dispelled with the triumph of the previews and particularly the opening night. By that time most of us were too exhausted to realise just how stupendous it had been. The following weeks, months and years showed us just what a gargantuan success and cult show *Wicked* had become.

And, of course, with that sort of attention you are required to do your share of interviews.

I've done quite a few interviews over the years and I really can't recall any horrors (although I know that they happen from time to time to other people). In fact, truth be told, I have been quite delighted with a great deal of them.

Interestingly, my favourite interviews have been on radio programmes. I am very fond of radio, besides as the saying goes, 'It doesn't matter how you wear your hair!' and this informality tends to create a relaxed atmosphere. If it is an in-depth sort of interview, say on the ABC (Australia's little sister to Auntie BBC) it can be very rewarding both for me and for the interviewer. Some interviewers, if they have done their research, can really delve into the finer points of my life. If I feel a connection with them, I can be quite revealing. If not, I choose my words carefully. Of course, most times on commercial radio or television interviews are for publicity purposes, an upcoming show or a charity event. In these cases, speed is of the essence to get the message across. Interviews for publications also depend on the research done by the journalist. In print, words need to be chosen carefully because irony and humour, so effectively conveyed by tone of voice and timing, often don't translate very well. I'm sorry to have to say that, in spite of the *vast* amount of easy-to-access information at everyone's fingertips nowadays, today's crop of young journalists almost always invariably lack the skills of their predecessors and the ability to research background, and, as a result, a really good interviewer is increasingly harder to find.

One interview I did enjoy was for *Wicked*, and you can find it here: www.youtube.com/watch?v=dEyr7GpONm8

We witnessed fans who followed us everywhere, all over Australia and even to New Zealand and South Korea. It was a phenomenon that never looked like tiring.

Amanda Harrison and Lucy Durack shone as Elphaba and Glinda. They were triumphant. As was Rob Guest as the Wizard. For me, the fabulous role of Madam Morrible was a gift if ever there was one.

I found playing Madam Morrible no more nor no less difficult than most of the characters I have had to play. In fact, I found her *most satisfying*. Perhaps the combination of imperiousness, craftiness and fabulous costuming made it all the easier. It is always very rewarding to play a Machiavellian type as opposed to a bland goodie. I think you will find that most actors love to play a baddie, or indeed someone who is their polar opposite.

The ensemble of *Wicked* consisted of a cast of extremely talented young performers. They were a dazzling collection of 'Triple Threats' … singing, dancing, acting with such aplomb.

After only three months, we were dealt a terrible blow. Beloved Rob Guest, one of the true gentlemen of show business, died very suddenly. On my way to a Wednesday matinee, I met the stage manager outside the stage door. She informed me that understudy, Rodney Dobson was going on as the Wizard. I found this very peculiar because Rob was the sort of performer that only something really drastic could keep from the stage. To add to my confusion, I was told that Kellie Dickerson, our musical director and Rob's partner would also be absent. I simply assumed that something deeply personal, perhaps family matter had taken place. But after the matinee we were informed by our producer, John Frost, that Rob had died following a massive stroke.

Our grief was immeasurable as we had all grown to love Rob. He was a fine and generous performer and I so enjoyed my brief time in his company. He was renowned as a warm, caring and funny man who was a great role model for young performers. He went out of his way to mentor and encourage them. To this day, in his honour, there exists The Rob Guest Endowment Award. This award is a scholarship providing assistance and support for the next generation of musical theatre performers, musicians and creatives.

So, dear Rob's memory lives on in a world he so loved.

The grief experienced by all of us was palpable as it was for the theatre community at large. To replace him was an unenviable task for the producers.

Eventually, the choice was made. Bert Newton was chosen to fill the role. My understanding, at the time, was that this appointment was to be for three months – it lasted for three years.

Bert Newton is an iconic TV star of many decades and much loved by the Australian public but in my opinion was not particularly well cast in the role. To me, the role required an actor able to inhabit the complex peculiarities of the Wizard. With respect, Bert had a larger than life personality and this, to me, overshadowed the Wizard beneath the makeup.

When I enquired as to the reason for his casting, the response was typical of producers the world over. 'He will put bums on seats.'

Interesting, I thought, as in all media advertising, no cast names were mentioned. Just the power of the word *Wicked* and the iconic logo filled the theatres.

Sadly, for three years, I found Bert's attitude to me off stage quite inappropriate thus making my working life with him uncomfortable, to say the least. Our Melbourne season continued on with the sort of success that this show enjoyed the world over.

After sixteen months it was time to pack up and move on to Sydney. My time in Melbourne was, as always, a joy. To be in a city I loved, working and being around friends who mean a lot to me was heaven.

Home to Sydney and more success followed us. It was going to be a bumper season in my home town.

Cast changes came and went, as happens in a long-running show. Some roles proved to be a little too challenging and were recast. The massive role of Elphaba had the greatest number of re-castings. This was a giant of a role requiring the utmost physical and vocal strength. Probably among the most demanding of musical theatre roles, it tested great performers the world over. Through all the cast changes, the joy and brilliance of the show still shone through and the crowds flocked to have the *Wicked* experience.

It was during the Sydney season that two great sadnesses befell me. One of my oldest friends died after a long illness. Ronaele Jones had been a friend since the early sixties and was an integral part of my life. I had known her first when she was a student, then through art school and finally she became one of the best wallpaper and fabric designers in the country. She was clever, witty and committed to the search for a better world. Highly critical of the status quo she railed against the injustices of the world. She took no bullshit from me or anyone for that matter and kept my feet firmly planted on terra firma.

Another loss during this time was dear Amanda Zachariah. Amanda and I had become firm friends when as a journalist, she was sent to interview me during the *Prisoner* years. We found so much in common to share – food, wine, humour, books, films and a love of life. Mandy came from a most interesting family headed by Harry, her father. The youngest sibling, Mandy had two sisters, Sue and Jane, both school teachers, and brother Richard, renowned journalist and media personality. Harry was a man I would have loved as a father. A teacher of many years standing in the Mr Chips fashion, he had taught several generations of boys at Brighton Boy's Grammar in Melbourne. My time in his company was always stimulating and challenging, he was truly one of life's great gentlemen. When Amanda married Graham, the love of her life, he, too became dear to me. His pain on losing Mandy was something that I am sure haunts him to this day.

This was a continuing for me of the cycle of sadness that comes when loved ones die. Alas it continues with regularity as the years roll by.

Into the Sydney season, on a Wednesday matinee day, I developed shortness of breath and rapid irregular heartbeat. A trip to a G.P. and then to a cardiologist saw me undergo a mountain of tests and then the diagnosis of atrial fibrillation. After a day or two it was back on stage and armed with the medications that have been my companions ever since. There is no doubt in my mind that this condition is genetic. Two grandmothers and a mother suffered a stroke. I also accept the fact that my long time drinking and smoking have also contributed enormously.

After a wonderful season of over a year in Sydney, I took myself off for another visit to the UK.

It's a great feeling to know that there was a job to come back to and that I had the money to indulge myself. Besides there was another Prisoner Fan Club event to do while there. This time it was in Birmingham and I was paired at the event with my on-screen nemesis Rita the Beater who in real life is gentle, caring, Glenda Linscott.

Also on the agenda in Birmingham was an appearance at the N.E.C. – The National Exhibition Centre. This was an incredible experience as hundreds of actors from all manner of TV shows met thousands of fans and posed for photos and signed autographs. It was a sight to behold, this vast arena venue with all sorts of weird and wonderful costumed fans paraded around. There were the Darth Vaders and the Luke Skywalkers, The Doctor Spocks and the Doctor Whos to name a few, all parading around as if auditioning for a role. It was hilarious but kind of weird to see so many obsessed people in the one place.

After Birmingham, I gave myself some treats in London. Although wintry, I still found the city enchanting. I immersed myself in the theatre. Shows such as *Warhorse*, *Deathtrap* with Simon Russell Beale; *The Country Girl* with Martin Shaw and Jenny Seagrove; *The Rivals* with Penelope Keith and Peter Bowles and Stephen Daldry's acclaimed revival *of An Inspector Calls*. My time was a feast of good theatre, shopping and great food. I will never let it be said that the Londoners don't have great restaurants. Well, once upon a time they didn't.

Then home for Christmas and more rehearsals before moving on to Brisbane. Curiously, on New Year's Eve while rehearsing, I noticed some swelling of my ankles and a shortness of breath. I went to my local G.P., who was concerned that I might get DVT (deep vein thrombosis) as a result of the long flight home. Tests carried out that afternoon showed a small abnormality on my lung. No time to do anything about it in Sydney so off I went to Brisbane armed with my x ray to be dealt with later.

No sooner had we settled in to the theatre and our digs than the heavens opened and then began one of the worst floods in Brisbane' history. I recall watching the water rise in the Brisbane river from my high-rise apartment, I watched water fill a building site excavation opposite and spill out and over the street. The CBD was like a ghost town and we seemed marooned. The theatre was deemed off limits as water had flooded the basement and the electrical equipment. Some thirty-five people died in that flood and over 200,000 people were affected. Damages came to around 2.38 billion dollars. There have been recriminations and blaming ever since.

We were sent back home until the raging waters subsided. Consequently, we didn't have the usual celebratory opening night. A very low-key opening saw us then embark on another great season. This show, I suspect, was just what the people of Queensland needed, and they came in their thousands.

When we were up and running, I followed up with the lung situation. During the day I had masses of tests. Lung function, blood, x-rays, CT scans – the lot. Then off to the theatre at night and back again next day for more tests. After a biopsy was performed, the diagnosis was an Adenocarcinoma.

An annoying little sucker sitting on the top of my left lung. The list of causes reads like a what's what of my dissolute life. No treatment. Surgery was the only option as it was very early stage and the removal of the upper lobe offers the best chance of cure.

So, in the capable hands of a wonderful surgeon, the operation was successful. Just the smallest scar near my left shoulder blade is the evidence of the surgeon's skill. I spent a week in that hospital, being very bolshie about my physiotherapy. Hours after the surgery I was toddling up and down the corridor complete with drips, bags and oxygen determined to get back to work ASAP.

When I was discharged I continued my rehab at the apartment complex. Swimming and treadmill work were my daily routine. However, all my determination was to no avail. In spite of my protestations I was repatriated back to Sydney in readiness for Adelaide. Looking back, I still maintain that I was ready to finish the Brisbane season and now wish that I had obtained a health certificate to that effect.

While out of the show in Brisbane, the wonderful Geraldine Turner was brought in as my replacement. Geb is a wonderful performer and a true star of musical theatre. I knew that Madam Morrible was in very good hands.

What I didn't count on though was the arrangement made without consulting me that Geraldine would alternate the role with me for a few weeks in Adelaide. I still maintain that this was an unnecessary expense on the part of the management. I was keeping up my fitness and felt more than capable of doing the eight shows a week.

The company's reason remains a mystery to me to this day.

Maybe they were just hedging their bets?

Being cautious?

Producers!

Towards the end of the Adelaide season, my difficult relationship with Bert Newton came to a head.

The final insult came when, on stage after the curtain call, speeches were being made regarding an audience bucket collection for a charity. As usual during these moments, Newton turned the moment into a 'comedy' routine. More often than not, I was the brunt of these attempts. This last time was too much. In front of a family audience of some 2000 people, he chose to joke about 'having' me. This was followed by the smutty double entendre, 'My moon in Uranus!' A gasp was audible from both cast and audience. A very feeble attempt at humour that fell very flat.

Standing beside him in front of some two thousand people at a family-oriented show, I was deeply humiliated by the crass comment. I stood my ground, when the temptation to walk off the stage was great, but when finally leaving the stage, I let fly with the anger that had been building up for three years. That was done, and I have not spoken to him since.

During the Brisbane season, I celebrated my 70th birthday. Much fuss was made by my colleagues and aside from the impending surgery, it was great to celebrate that milestone whilst being in a hit show. I guess that's all actors can wish for as we get older, to be in work, doing what we love and in the company of like-minded chums. I felt blessed.

Little did I realise how much the aging process was catching up with me, physically. The decline of my right hip had most certainly been exacerbated by the myriad stairs at the Regent Theatre and the extraordinary weight of my costumes. As the Adelaide season progressed, the niggling pain persisted. Momentary relief came with massage, acupuncture and mild exercise, but the Perth season loomed.

Once again, a sell-out season, but towards the end of the run I was relying on a walking stick, on and off stage. Our extremely creative Props Master, Bruce Ferguson, supplied me with a most elegant walking stick, befitting my ultra glamourous costumes. It was a prop that I never expected to use – and did I make a meal of it! That damned stick became an integral part of my performance! Such a ham!

Recently, Bruce reminded me of those days, 'You were in such pain, and I gave you a walking stick to match your costume. I was always amazed as you stood in the wings awaiting your entrance, hunched over with pain. At your cue to enter, you straightened up and walked on stage with audience and most of the cast none the wiser. On your exit, you would grab hold of someone to help you to your dressing room. Fabulous!'

On arrival back home in Sydney it was decided that I needed a hip replacement operation. This was then organised, and I left the company for the duration of the Singapore season.

Operation done. Rehab done and by early 2012 I was rearing to go again, damned costumes and all.

I found Seoul to be a very upmarket city. Fine shops and restaurants abounded. I found great book shops, galleries and craft shops. The walking tracks were amazing. Dotted across the city in parks, the walkers could avail themselves of exercise equipment featured in those parks. It was great to walk and exercise out in the open even if the pollution sometimes was a bit off putting. Elderly Koreans, carefully shaded from the sun, indulged in the walking and gentle work outs. I found it all extremely beneficial in light of my recent surgery.

Once again, the cult status of *Wicked* continued. Enormous, packed houses and crowds of fans at the stage door after every performance.

We were there from May to October and on August 31, the news came that my darling mother Crissie had died in her sleep. Aged ninety-five, she lived independently in her apartment. As it was a Friday, she would have been to the hairdresser for her weekly 'do', cooked her dinner, watched the Friday night football and then gone to bed to read. When my brother called in the next morning, she had her glasses on and the book across her chest as if she had just dozed off.

My feelings were very difficult to process or even describe. How does one describe the emotions that come with the loss of a parent? Yes, I felt a great sense of loss, of sadness, of the end of a life that had been the cornerstone of my existence. My relationship with my mother was as fractious yet loving as any mother/daughter relationship. I always felt that she loved me, but she was never very demonstrative with that love. Perhaps it was a generational thing as she, being the youngest in her family, had probably not had hugely overt displays of affection lavished upon her.

She gave me freedom and I knew the boundaries but eventually I flouted them as any rebellious teenager would. I would describe her parenting as gently strict, but there was never any harshness about her and although I did see a caustic side to her when she levelled criticism at adults I don't recall ever being slapped by her as was the common practice in those days.

My mother had a great sense of humour and at times could be quite the clown.

An incident that I have never forgotten occurred one day when I was about nine or ten. My stepfather was working in the garden and I was doing whatever kids do. For some reason he gently chastised me and when he turned away, I pulled a face and poked my tongue out at him. Mum had witnessed this from the kitchen window and came racing out brandishing a wooden spoon ready to give me a good whack. I took off with her giving chase. Suddenly, the elastic in her knickers gave way and her bloomers fell to her ankles. This put a stop to any punishment that might have come my way and caused the three of us to collapse with hysterical laughter.

As far as my chosen career was concerned, I felt that she was proud of me but there was always a sneaking suspicion on my part that she wished I had a 'real' job.

My one regret regarding Crissie is that I never had her manage my money. She was a whiz at budgeting, saving and planning. I would be in a better financial position today had I heeded her.

I was comforted by the fact that my mother had lived her life on her own terms. Having been widowed at such a young age, alone and responsible for a young life, she moved on to a strange new town, made a good life for us both and found happiness again when she remarried and when my brother came along.

I think she was a remarkable woman and like many of her generation, unsung.

Towards the end, her life didn't seem to hold much joy for her except in the company of grandchildren and great grandchildren. Old friends had long gone and her mobility was compromised. I am comforted by the fact that she lived her life well, she had given, and received love and respect.

As the year 2012 turned into 2013, the world saw the premier of *Wentworth*, the reimagining of *Prisoner: Cell Block H*. It is, in my opinion, a most worthy exploration into the dark world of female prison life. I personally find it thrilling and am in awe of the performances. I am sure that many *Prisoner* fans who are now fans of *Wentworth* would want to know my opinion of the new Ferguson. As I have stated many times, I am grateful to have had the chance to create a character that seems to have become such a world-wide talking point. It gives me great pleasure to see the recreation of that character in the hands of the remarkable Pamela Rabe. I have already indicated my respect and fondness for Pamela, both as a friend and as a colleague but I feel that her interpretation of Ferguson has taken it to new heights. I appreciate that my version in the eighties was considered scary but the changed attitudes and production values of today have enabled Pamela and the cast to leap both the technical and the thematic hurdles that existed in the eighties.

The stories are grittier, the characters meaner and the whole thing is riskier.

I love its gutsiness.

Meanwhile, I was now deeply ensconced in the world of Oz – a completely different realm altogether.

For the seven-year duration of *Wicked*, the touring schedules included 'off' times when distances between venues ruled the transportation of the gigantic set, costumes and all the equipment that goes with such a leviathan show.

Sometimes, these breaks lasted for several months and the opportunity to enjoy down time at home or on holiday was very welcome as the security of the next season was guaranteed.

During some of these breaks, I caught up with family and friends, saw shows, renovated my house and sometimes took an overseas holiday.

After Seoul we had quite a long break before heading to New Zealand, a country of which I am very fond. Since 1966 I have made a number of trips 'across the ditch' and I have always enjoyed the experience. I have often admired the people of that country for stances taken on such issues as human rights, whaling, nuclear weapons and the environment. In 1984, David Lange took a stand with his non-nuclear defence policy, denying entry to New Zealand of nuclear ships. This action saw him swept to victory in the General Election thus becoming the then youngest Prime Minister of the 20th century.

Once, having to make a speech at an anti-nuclear rally in Melbourne, I cited Lange's policy in regard to the Pacific region and likened his strength to that of a 'David and Goliath' struggle as he stood up to powerful nuclear nations.

For a tiny country, New Zealand has always punched above its weight on important global issues and I have long admired the people of Aotearoa.

Our season in Auckland was as successful as everywhere else and even allowed for a little leisure to enjoy the delights of that city. We finished in November of 2013 and headed home for Christmas.

Then the walls came tumbling down.

CHAPTER THIRTEEN

TUMBLEDOWN

I had motored to the North Coast of NSW to spend Christmas with my family, and then on to the Queensland Sunshine Coast to celebrate the engagement of my grandson, Daniel to his beautiful Brittany. Of course, I am biased, but they really are a heavenly couple, perfectly matched and nowadays they are the wonderful parents of my great-granddaughter, Amelia.

While in Queensland I spent time exploring and spending time with old friends, Rainee Skinner and Gary Scale along with their partners.

Rainee Skinner is the actress sister of my old friend Carole Skinner and long-time family friend.

Garry Scale a friend since his graduation from NIDA in the seventies. A fun, loyal friend who many years ago, created a family legend. He was ostensibly minding Caitlin, my daughter and a school friend of hers. They were probably about fourteen or fifteen at the time. Garry decided to take the girls out one night. To a movie? For a milkshake? No! He took them to Patches, a gay night club to see a drag show! A funny side to this story is that quite a number of drag queens knew Caitlin, made a fuss and generally behaved like a bunch of old aunties.

Finally, on New Year's Eve I set off on the long journey back to Sydney.

About 500 kms from home, my phone rang and when a suitable moment came, I pulled to the side of the highway to return the call.

The message was gut-wrenching as I listened to the voice of a detective in Melbourne wishing to contact me 'in regard to allegations of sexual assault in the eighties'.

Never in my wildest dreams could I have imagined this bombshell that hit me.

Even as I write now, I find it hard to put into words what I felt at that moment. My response was of utter disbelief and as I tried to maintain some semblance of calm and dignity I could feel the bile rising in my throat. After assuring the detective that I would contact her after the holiday, I staggered out of my car and, on the side of the highway, I threw up. I felt enormous pain, despair and isolation as I sat in my car, holiday traffic zooming by trying to comprehend what had just been thrown at me.

As I gathered my thoughts, I contemplated the long journey still to come. It was, without doubt the most nightmarish ride of my life as I tried desperately to concentrate.

Finally, at home, I didn't know what to do, who to call. It was New Year's Eve and most people I could have confided in were out celebrating.

Eventually, I phoned my good friend Geoffrey Satchell who was at his holiday home in far North Queensland. Geoff's long-time partner Robbie had been a police prosecutor and I felt that he could best advise me. As luck would have it, a house guest, Sue, was also there. She, too, had been a prosecutor.

Through my hysteria and tears they both advised that I should do nothing at this point except to make it clear that I would cooperate after seeking legal advice.

Thus began two and half years of carrying this hideous burden.

In January of 2014 it was off to the Philippines. A great black cloud hung over me but in spite of that this was a new adventure and I was determined to make the most of it.

I had never had any real desire to visit this country but the joy of being in a long-running show brought with it the excitement of new lands.

Manila is an extraordinary city and like many other Asian cities, the evidence of inequality is glaringly obvious.

We stayed in a five-star hotel with security guards at every corner. To access the hotel, buses, cars and taxis were required to stop and a search of the undercarriage was carried out and then there was a full security check at the entrance of persons and bags. Although the same personnel searched us day and night for all those weeks, it made no difference, we were subjected to the routine on every entry to the hotel.

The luxury of the hotel was in sickening contrast to the poverty on the streets nearby. Along the waterfront highway, on a wide nature strip, men, women, children and dogs could be seen sleeping rough. Begging in the streets was epidemic and in contrast the surrounding high-end shopping centres carried all the luxury goods one would find in any large western city.

A security check was even necessary on entering the stores. While waiting for a taxi after some shopping, I noticed several heavily armed guards patrolling the pavement. I assumed that they were military personnel. No, the backs of their jackets were emblazoned with the word 'TRAFFIC'. They were armed sufficiently to take out a small village. Strangest traffic wardens I have ever encountered.

The theatre where we played was a little way from the hotel and in the interests of comfort and safety we were transported back and forth by bus. I wasn't too sure about the safety aspect as several drivers persisted in watching television on small screens near the steering wheel as they manoeuvred the bus through hell for leather traffic.

The Cultural Center of the Philippines was the name of the theatre complex where we played. It was a large fortress-like, government-owned building. I think it safe to say that in architectural styles it was 'Brutalist' and wouldn't have been out of place in Hitler's Germany, probably designed by Albert Speer.

It was, however, from the Marcos era and at the time of our visit I understood that Mme Imelda Marcos still attended the occasional opening night. Sad to say, I didn't see her at ours so I'm unable to describe which shoes of the thousands of pairs she is reported to own were being worn.

I had been advised by friend Peter Whitford that high tea at the legendary Manila Hotel was a must. As with Raffles in Singapore or the Peninsula in Hong Kong, I looked forward to some of the colonial elegance of bygone days.

Yes, there was music, but not a tinkling piano or a gentle string quartet, just Muzak. Indeed, there were sandwiches and cakes – dry and boring – and as for the tea? No silver tea service with all the accoutrements of tea making, just a few tea BAGS in a very ordinary pot!

My companion for this culinary disaster was our 'props' master, Bruce Ferguson, himself no stranger to some of the finer things in life. We were hysterical with laughter in spite of our disappointment. So much for trying to relive bygone days.

The season was, as usual, a triumph. Fans gathered before and after the show and on our final night the street had to be cordoned off to accommodate the multitude who had come to say goodbye.

Throughout my stay, no matter how hard I tried, the thought of what awaited me in Melbourne weighed heavily.

I confided in a couple of friends, Ryan Sheppard and Tom Handley and also Kellie Ritchie, our makeup supervisor. After all this time together, Kellie had become very dear to me and she displayed her usual pragmatic yet sympathetic manner.

In the company of these dear friends and our company manager, Bec Windsor, I was able to enjoy some of the fun that goes with being on tour. Days by the pool, nights off and some fine dining all helped not only to pass the time but occasionally to free my mind.

March arrived, and it was time to head for home. This time a return season in Melbourne was scheduled. Six years after *Wicked*'s extraordinary debut we were going back. Unfortunately to the dreaded Regent Theatre and all those stairs but happily, a new Wizard. The great Reg Livermore was to take over the role. As a long-time admirer of this superb performer, I was most excited at the prospect of working with him. I certainly wasn't disappointed. Not only is Reg a master of his craft, he is a most entertaining man. We had such a good time. We shared gossip, books, newspapers and swapped stories. We railed together against injustices in the world and poo-pooed the politicians who really irritated us. He proved to be not just a great Wizard, but a dear friend and I became very fond of him.

And all the while, hanging over my head like the Sword of Damocles was the upcoming interview with Victoria Police.

Yet again, *Wicked* proved to be a record-breaking show. For quite a while the smooth running of the production had been in the hands of Karen Johnson-Mortimer, my friend from the *Irene* days some forty years ago. Karen's professional life's experiences had carved out a successful career for her both as actor and director. Under her guidance, the superior quality of the show remained intact. Often, a long-running show can get a little tired, but I don't believe for one moment that was the case with *Wicked*. Karen's eye for detail, her unerring good taste and empathy kept us all going. In spite of injuries and personal problems, the cast morale and the quality of performances was in the main due to her.

It was good, socially, to settle back into Melbourne. I took up residence in colourful St. Kilda once again. My spare time, in the main, seemed to be once again taken up with physiotherapy sessions, thanks to those damn stairs and the heavy costumes.

Then the day arrived when I went to Police Headquarters for my interview.

'Assisting with enquiries' is a much-touted phrase but my recollection is that I was actually arrested. I really can't recall the exact words, but I was cautioned, photographed but not fingerprinted. It appears that the machine was out of order and the investigating detective didn't think that I should do the ink method.

How considerate.

Having no experience with such things, I was naturally apprehensive and certainly nervous in spite of the fact that I knew I had done nothing wrong. Throughout the lengthy interview and detailed questioning, the female detective was courteous and respectful. Her colleague was a little brusque but then maybe it was the 'good cop, bad cop' routine. Or had I watched too much crime TV?

The allegations against me were of the sexual assault variety. My accuser had been, in 1985, a teenage fan of *Prisoner*. At the time a request was made by an employee at Channel 10 for me to visit this young person who was in a psychiatric facility. I obliged. Nowadays, I would never be allowed to visit alone. I would have been accompanied by a publicist. But times were different then and as I had visited many fans in their homes or in hospitals, I didn't think twice about it.

My memory of that visit decades ago is a little hazy and although I didn't pry, I realised that she was a troubled young person. I do recall inviting her to my home for a few hours respite from the institution. Permission was obtained, and I collected her one Sunday afternoon. I showed her around my house and she was given free rein. As I prepared a meal in the kitchen, she watched videos and played with my dog and occasionally chatted with me as I worked. I didn't learn about her problems and nor did I ask.

Unbeknown to me, she had helped herself to some liquor that was in my dining room.

After some time, I realised that she was affected by the alcohol and I decided to end the visit. I gave her a sweater as the afternoon had turned chilly (I was questioned about this as if it were some sort of sinister act) and then I put her in a taxi to go back to the institution.

This was probably not the best idea, but I had consumed a couple of glasses of wine while cooking and thought better of driving.

There was no further contact with this young person and my life went on as usual. I was not about to make a lifelong friend of a disturbed young girl. Her life, her problems were for her to resolve. It was not the duty of a fictional being from her favourite television show to be part of her life.

The questioning was extremely detailed, the lay out of my house, the type of car I drove, the type of dog I owned. There were even questions as to whether I had taken her upstairs. Of course I had, to show her around my house and where the lavatory was! All these questions were, no doubt, to corroborate my accusers' statement. Her claims, apparently, had been made in mid-2013. My cynical mind recalled that around that time cases against Rolf Harris and Robert Hughes regarding alleged sexual misconduct had come into the public arena. A little warning bell was sounding in my head.

After a very long session of questioning, I was free to go. I thought that would be the end of the matter.

How wrong I was.

The rest of my time in Melbourne was clouded by the fact that I didn't know what my accuser looked like. Was she a danger to me.? It was very easy to gain access to me, at the stage door, the car park or even the alley that I had to walk through to get to my apartment. So, my every move caused a moment of caution on my part. Or was I just being paranoid?

Soon it was time to return to Sydney for yet another season. I left Melbourne with a meniscus tear in my left knee. The result of a slip on wet pavement in Auckland followed by a crash on stage a week later. Both times affecting the left knee. So, the break between Melbourne and Sydney required a quick knee surgery and then back on stage.

I guess that's life when the aging process takes over.

The Sydney season was yet another success, in spite of cast changes and health issues. I revelled in the continuing joy of working with Reg.

When time came to move on the Brisbane, I was saddened by the fact that Reg was not coming with us. However, I was in for a most pleasant surprise. His replacement turned out to be Simon Gallaher. I didn't know Simon personally, but I was well aware of his illustrious career. A gifted musician, and performer, he had shot to fame years before as a very young man on *The Mike Walsh Show*. Singing and playing piano, he fast became the darling of the 'blue rinse' set. For many years now, he has achieved enormous success as a producer, director and performer.

Simon's 'Wizard' was very different to Reg. Where Reg played the character as a lithe, conniving manipulator, Simon was appealingly avuncular. I loved being on stage with both versions. In each instance, I found my own performance being enhanced by playing opposite them.

Brisbane was Simon's home town and he was an instant hit. I was amused by the fact that our opening performance was actually held in the late afternoon instead of the usual 8 pm show. This late 'matinee' was followed by cocktails and canapes in the parkland of the theatre at dusk – a perfect time in this sub-tropical setting and extremely appreciated by the older audience members who were somewhat past the 'Rave Party' scene – myself included.

Into the season I received the phone call that I had been dreading. I had, in fact, almost put it out of my mind as so much time had passed.

The Melbourne detective who had originally notified me of the accusations against me informed me that the DPP (Department of Public Prosecutions) had deemed that there was a case to be made. She then informed me that I needed a lawyer to whom she could serve the relevant papers, as a magistrate's court hearing was imminent.

Again, the bottom fell out of my world. Initially, I felt enormous panic and helplessness. Then logic took over. I needed legal counsel, but where did I find that in Melbourne when I was in Brisbane. Once again, I reached out to my friends Geoffrey and Robbie. Bearing in mind that Robbie and his friend Sue had not only been police officers but also prosecutors.

They recommended a former colleague with similar background, ex police, ex prosecutor and now a defence lawyer. His name was Stephen Preece and via a phone call, he agreed to take my case.

All was then set in motion for him to represent me and to appear at the forthcoming Magistrate's Court appearance on my behalf.

Fearing media attention if the court lists were noticed, the management urged me to take time off in case there was a backlash. As I had nothing to hide or be ashamed of, I was rather disappointed with this edict. However, I complied and then drove south to my stay with my daughter.

Stephen was successful in having the case adjourned, there were no repercussions from the media and so after a week I was permitted to return to the show. A second application for adjournment was successful and, so far, it had all gone unnoticed by the media.

Wicked rolled on to Perth and my time there was made all the more bearable by the company of Simon and his wife Lisa who were of great comfort to me as were other cast colleagues. My mind was constantly abuzz with what I was to face in the near future.

Finally, we reached the end of 'The Yellow Brick Road' and the great caravan that was *Wicked* came to a close. It had been a phenomenal six years and some 2000 performances. In spite of my absences I managed to clock up just over 1600 performances. Not bad for an old girl!

So ended an amazing period of show business history – a time when romances blossomed, weddings and funerals happened, babies were born, and real estate was bought. It was fascinating to be part of the ups and downs of this little world. Young talent grew and progressed to bigger things and old talent found affirmation of their worth.

Once back home in Sydney, weeks passed without incident then one evening a phone call rocked my world yet again. A young journalist from my least-favourite newspaper chain, News Corp, phoned to ask if I had any comment to make regarding my forthcoming court appearance. My response was abrupt, I simply hung up.

Quite shaken by the call, I tried to put the consequences of such an intrusion out of my mind. Although I was fully aware of the type of journalism that came from these newspapers, nothing could have prepared me for the avalanche of vulgar, cruel outpourings that were to come my way.

The next day I answered a call at my front door. As I lived in a semi-rural area, knocks on the front door were rare – except perhaps for the occasional Jehovah's Witness. My friends usually, drove up to my garage and came into the house through the back door.

Imagine my shock when I opened the door to a very young, very rude so-called journalist from the ghastly *Daily Telegraph*, from the same stable as the Melbourne *Herald-Sun* and equally sensationalist.

He, like his colleague on the phone the day before, wanted comments regarding the forthcoming court case. Out of the corner of my eye I spotted a photographer some 150 metres away with his long-range lens trained on my front door. My response to this invasion of privacy was to point out that they were trespassing and then closed the door. This intruding snoop warned me that the story was going to break in the next morning's edition.

I went into a state of fearful panic. I paced, I cried, I ranted like a mad woman. Finally, I could stand it no longer and phoned a friend who lived nearby, and I was immediately collected and whisked away to the privacy of her home where in the caring company of my friends, Lloyd and Gail, I waited for the storm that was about to break.

Even now, as I write about that awful period, I feel my heart beat a little faster, my stomach churn and my palms a little sweaty. There is just so much to convey, and I fear that I won't be able to do justice to the story I have to tell. Will I remember the details? Will I be able to explain exactly how I felt at the time? Will the anger, frustration and hurt be conveyed? I can only try. My impulse at the moment of writing is to run away, read a book, watch mindless television, go for a walk, anything to avoid reliving those days.

When the story broke the next morning, all areas of the media had a feeding frenzy. They all were like vultures feeding on carrion. In almost every instance there was reference to the type of character that I had played in *Prisoner*. 'Sadistic', 'Lesbian' and 'Freak' were just a few of the expletives used. I found it telling in particular that 'Lesbian' was obviously meant as some sort of slur. When vision was displayed, print or TV they were always images of Joan Ferguson. Yes, the name Maggie Kirkpatrick was there of course, but mostly in a cursory fashion. It became clear that it was the nefarious *lesbian* prison warder who was on trial.

There were areas of the media from whom I expected gutter journalism but my heart nearly broke when the usually circumspect broadcaster the esteemed ABC had, on a news bulletin running the story, shown footage from *Prisoner* which featured me, as Joan Ferguson, in handcuffs being led away by two policemen – vision from a long-ago episode, yet being shown as if it were the real thing. So even the poison of gutter journalism had invaded the national broadcaster.

While at my friend's house, media crews had taken up residence outside my house harassing my neighbours – in fact, behaving in the way we have all come to expect. To this day my heart sinks when I see people, innocent or guilty being pursued by yapping journalists and camera crews, invading their space and privacy as I have learned – the hard way.

Several kilometres away I was fielding calls from family and friends far and wide, from the UK and even from Jackie Weaver in Los Angeles. The news, *of course*, was all over the internet. There were some areas of the media who, for whatever reason, had my phone number – probably from the days when we were friends! Interviews and statements were being requested. I tried to refuse as politely as I could and that wasn't easy.

My daughter Caitlin and my grandchildren Megan and Daniel were, naturally, very distressed but loving and supportive as indeed they had been when I had told them a year before. My brother Adrian and his family were also quick to jump to my defence when social media took up the story. Naturally, with that outlet everyone has an opinion, if only to make themselves feel important. I have nothing to do with all that Facebook stuff. From where I stand, it has some good points in enabling people to connect but on the whole, it appears to be a destructive force in the hands of desperate, narcissistic people. I am happy to communicate by email, phone or snail mail with the people who matter.

I allowed myself a small smile when I realised that the snooping media had missed the two occasions when this matter had already been before the court. After a few days, the heat subsided. No doubt there was fresh prey to be harassed.

My next obstacle, August 19, loomed large. That was the date set for the trial to be held in Melbourne.

CHAPTER FOURTEEN

TRIAL AND CONFABULATION

A pre-appearance conference was held, and I finally came face to face with my lawyer Stephen Preece and the barrister whom he had briefed, Justin Hannebery. These two young men held my fate in their hands and they immediately instilled in me a feeling of hope and confidence and I really felt that this nightmare would be over very soon.

Two witnesses were called. My dear friend Geoff Satchell who had known me for some forty years and Jo-Anne Richardson who had known me for a similar length of time. As a teenager, due to her family situation, Jo opted to live with me and Caitlin while she was studying. As a teenager at the time living at close quarters with me she was a perfect witness given the nature of the charges. She also kindly attributed her success in life, which was considerable, to me for giving her the space to follow her dreams.

The short walk from chambers to the Magistrates Court was a nightmare. Every television news or current affairs report that I had seen came at me like a herd of stampeding cattle. Cameras and microphones shoved in my face, inane questions shouted at me. All the ugliness of media madness was there in front of me. The urge to lash out at them was strong. Thankfully some innate sense of dignity prevailed as I made my way to the courtroom flanked by Justin and Stephen.

Once there, another surprise awaited me. My accuser had not only a closed court in which to give her statement, but a whiteboard screen was erected in front of her so that she was only visible to the magistrate. I have no idea what the purpose of that was, but I would have thought that a mature woman, as she was, would have the courage to face even a closed court.

My two witnesses were called and gave very good accounts of their knowledge of, and relationship with, me. My video interview of the year before was presented in evidence and I was excused from taking the stand. My accuser's witnesses were her husband (for what reason I couldn't fathom as he hadn't known her thirty years previously), a childhood friend and her psychiatrist from all those years ago.

I was a little baffled by the presence of her husband, as she was now in her mid-forties and he couldn't possibly have been a reliable witness to the accusations but apparently she intimated to him that the alleged assault had taken place. He claimed that the information came to him during some sort of emotional crisis between them.

The psychiatrist, although summoned by the prosecution, actually turned out to be a favourable witness on my account due to his testimony as to her mental condition at the time of the alleged offence. I believe that as a young girl she had suffered a number of disturbing episodes in her life which necessitated intervention. In the psychiatrist's summing up he conceded that she had been a very disturbed girl. I was never privy to those reasons or causes, suffice to say that his testimony made the accusation a lot clearer.

We were then adjourned until the following day when the magistrate would deliver his findings.

After a very restless night, I returned to the court and once again ran the gauntlet of the circling pack. Unknown to me, my team, Justin and Stephen didn't have a great deal of confidence in the magistrate, one Peter Mealy, who was known to be harsh and unyielding. So, as I stood for his verdict I could hardly believe my ears.

GUILTY.

Not only that verdict but I was *castigated* by him for not showing any remorse and if the case had not been an historical one, he would have jailed me. As my mind became a blur the words rang through the roaring in my ears, 'no remorse', 'sex offenders register', 'community service' and 'DNA sample'.

I don't have words to describe just what I felt at that moment.

I know I felt physically ill and didn't know whether I would faint or scream. Stephen, Justin and my good friend Wendy Becher who had been in court both days, took me to an anteroom so that I might compose myself. Wendy rang Caitlin with the hideous news and Caitlin, in her shocked state, asked if paramedics were nearby as my heart condition gave her cause for alarm. However, I wasn't about to check out just yet and as my tears dried, Stephen and I went through the immediate process of lodging an appeal. We learned that this would be heard in early December.

The general consensus of opinion at that time was that Peter Mealy's findings and remarks were way off the mark. As for not showing remorse, how could I when I *knew* that I had done nothing wrong?

Leaving the courthouse, I was once again subjected to the barrage of media. Once again, their aggressive behaviour and puerile questions made me feel like lashing out and once again I resisted the temptation.

I found the next twenty-four hours very difficult to get through. Travelling home, I felt that all eyes were on me as I made my way through the airport, on to the plane and back to Sydney airport. Paranoia was having a field day. Occasionally on that journey, strangers offered me their sympathy and that was a small step in regaining some dignity. Travelling alone under these circumstances I felt isolated and vulnerable like I never have before.

I understand that social media went into some sort of overdrive. Apparently, there were a few cruel and negative comments, but overwhelming support was in abundance. Fans, friends and colleagues seemed to rally in support of me. My family fielded and protected me from any negativity and my local community showed me enormous compassion and support. Even strangers gave vent to their anger over the verdict.

In spite of the impending appeal, I still had to go through another ordeal at a local police station. I had to report so that my DNA sample could be obtained, my passport confiscated, and my name added to the sex offenders register.

The ignominy I felt about this was lessened somewhat by the attitude of the officer dealing with the case. He was empathetic and treated me with dignity and respect. I am forever indebted to him for that kindness.

Now began the four-month wait to the appeal hearing. A long-planned holiday to the USA seemed in doubt, but my passport was handed back to me and I was free to take that trip. Although I wasn't too sure what sort of company I would be for my two friends, but Craig Bennett and Craig Murchie are very dear to me and this was, after all, a trip of a lifetime.

Throughout my life I have been blessed with wonderful friends. Some have been in my life for six decades and although not nearby, they are only a phone call away. All have enriched my life. Sadly, some dear friends are no longer with me. Death, it seems, doesn't discriminate. Young, middle-aged and old, these friends might have now gone from my life, leaving a void, but also treasured memories.

An enduring (and endearing) friendship is the one that I have with Craig Bennett and his partner Craig Murchie. Though somewhat younger than I am, they are 'old souls' and have been a source of great fun and love for nearly thirty years. Like all relationships we have had our glitches and differences but nothing that hasn't been overcome with a few tears, patience and the odd apology.

I can't imagine my life without them in it.

Originally, I had met Craig Bennett back in the eighties during *Prisoner* days. He was a showbiz journalist and in 1985 was launching a celebrity cookbook. This event, full of TV stars and personalities, was to be held in the garden of his parent's home on Sydney's North Shore. I was flown up from Melbourne for the event, managed to trash myself the night before and spent the afternoon comatose with a monumental hangover.

However, it was in 1992 that we were brought together again. As chance would have it, we lived in the same street in the Sydney suburb of Rozelle and before long a well-worn path seemed to emerge from the comings and goings of us both to each other's house.

Flamboyant celebrity Bernard King was a mutual friend and Craig intimated to me that he had fallen on less than salubrious times. As his birthday was imminent, we decided to host a birthday luncheon for him. Both Craig and I were somewhat depleted of funds (and work) but with a little imagination we managed to create a respectable menu. Guests were invited, among them two of the funniest women around, the late Lois Ramsey and Judith McGrath, always an asset at any table.

So, food was prepared, as I recall we were poaching salmon in champagne. The table set, guests arrived, drinks were served, and we waited for Bernard, the guest of honour.

We waited and we waited and we waited.

Finally, he deigned to show up, having already been celebrating elsewhere. He had in tow a group of free loaders he had gathered along the way. Naturally, they were very good-looking young men. A dash to the kitchen saw Craig and me dividing the salmon into smaller pieces, putting extra spuds in the pot and, somehow, we managed to feed them all. Talk about 'loaves and fishes' Unforgivably, Bernard's entourage consisted of monumental bores. But humour won the day and many a quip twixt sip and lip saw us through with flying colours.

Some of my happiest times with the Craigs have been bush walking and gathering rock orchids and elk horns, gardening, cooking, eating and enjoying good wines or simply stretched out on couches binging on old Hollywood movies of the 30s, 40s and 50s.

The story about Bernard is just one of myriad, mad incidents that have peppered our friendship.

Another silly moment occurred when we were to give a dinner party. Having over indulged the night before, Craig Bennett and I were languishing (our word for hungover and recovering) on sofas in the living room. The front door open and in walked Sarah Kemp and her two dogs. She had been invited to dinner, but this was three o'clock in the afternoon! Along with the dogs she was clutching her contribution to dinner, an open bottle of wine, contents half consumed.

Our reaction to her arrival was less than polite. 'Christ, Sarah, you're four hours early, take the dogs for a fucking walk!' Of course, when she did do just that, we collapsed in hysterics and then proceeded to think about the dinner menu.

Really silly events have peppered our years together, too numerous to remember and perhaps they are lost in a fog of good times and long lunches.

In 2013, during a break from *Wicked*, we took a holiday to Europe, the three of us. First stop was London, just forty-eight hours, time enough for a couple of delicious meals and a matinee of the great Helen Mirren in the play *An Audience*. What a special experience that was! To witness (from five rows back in the stalls!) this great actress playing Queen Elizabeth the Second from her ascension to the throne to the present day. Meetings with all her Prime Ministers, beginning with Winston Churchill and ending with David Cameron (the then P.M.) It was a delight never to be forgotten.

Then we were off to Ireland. Travelling with us was a good friend of the boys from Los Angeles, Pamela Godfrey – for many years a noted publicist in Hollywood who had worked on many major productions. She had just recently returned to the UK after the death of her father and set up Pamela Godfrey Marketing and Publicity. She has since been in involved in many high-profile projects including the film, *Hotel Mumbai*.

The four of us arrived in Cork and first motored to the very pretty fishing village of Dingle – quaint buildings painted in bright colours around a small harbour with bobbing fishing boats. Naturally, a fabulous sea food dinner was the order of our first day. With Craig Murchie at the wheel, we motored all around the south west of that beautiful country. Kinsale, Killarney, The Ring of Kerry. In the rain, the boys managed to kiss the Blarney Stone. I gave it a miss. Besides being almost physically impossible for this old body to do, I figured that after fifteen years of marriage to an Irishman I'd had my fair share of blarney.

We continued on our travels with much hilarity, good food and the odd Guinness.

Time came to say goodbye to Pamela and head for Milan. I was so excited to be returning to Italy, and this time with friends to share the delight.

I had never been to Milan, so it was a special treat for me and I wasn't disappointed. Such a stylish city, but then what city in Italy isn't stylish? We visited the magnificent Duomo, had Camparis in the Piazza, right next to the building where Campari was invented. We spent our evenings sampling the delicious food at various cafés along the canal. As it was summer, the bars, restaurants and piazzas were full of holiday makers. I shopped and shopped and shopped. I bought almost a complete summer wardrobe when I found a designer, Elena Miro, who had a vast range of stylish 'plus' sizes.

A visit to the Da Vinci Last Supper was an awe-inspiring experience. That something so simple could delight for so many years.

After Milan it was on to Como by train and then by ferry to Bellagio across Lake Como. What a breathtaking vista from the lake, the beautiful villas dotted around the majestic mountains rising on all sides. Even though it was summer, the highest peaks still had traces of snow.

Bellagio is picture-postcard beautiful, as were our suites. Just a couple of days taking in the beauty of Bellagio and then it was back to Como, but not before we had taken a trip around the lake in the snazziest speed boat. All gleaming brass and shining timber. It gave us a chance to really see the mansions along the foreshores. The villas along the shores of Lake Como can only be described as lavish beyond belief. Manicured gardens, sumptuous modern or traditional architecture. Opulence Plus!

Richard Branson's estate is amazing as was George Clooney's but sadly, we didn't see either of them. Perhaps our invitations to visit are in the mail? Ah, well, next time.

So, by train to Florence. Train travel in Italy is certainly different to my experiences of nearly thirty years before. Smooth travel, gourmet food and fast, smoothly fast.

The boys had not been to Florence before, so I was more than happy to suggest some highlights for them. This time we were in an apartment right in the centre of the city, so we had everything at our finger tips. Naturally, I told them about the Uffizi, the Duomo, the Pitti Palace and the Galleria dell'Accademia where I was once again smitten by the beauty of Michelangelo's

David and the drama of the Prisoners or the Slaves. The boys, being avid gardeners were delighted with the Boboli Gardens. Our time of exploring in Florence also included a visit to Dante's house and church and a personal guided walking tour at twilight. Points of historical interest, old and new, such as Ferragamo's original shop and factory, this appealed to the shoe lover in me and along the way we sampled local wines at various wine shops or enoteca.

The next morning it was time to move on by train to Naples then car to Sorrento.

An elegant hotel, fine food and breathtaking views of the Bay of Naples and Mount Vesuvius awaited us. My first swim in the Mediterranean took place way, way down from the cliff top to a beach that mainly consisted of decking, chairs, umbrellas and personal service, all for a price, *naturally*. The water was cold, choppy, salty but wonderfully invigorating.

There wasn't a lot to do in Sorrento, we were just three of the multitude of summer holiday makers. So we swam, shopped and ate fabulous food – all manner of amazing sea food from the Mediterranean. Mostly enjoyed al Fresco on the terrace overlooking the bay with amazing mansions all around, many, apparently, owned by wealthy Russians and with superb views of the Bay of Naples and Mt Vesuvius.

Sunday, we were off on the ferry to Capri. Another very crowded, very expensive holiday destination. Despite all that, there is no denying the beauty of that part of Italy. The amazing blue of the water, the lushness of the gardens and the elegance of the hotels and mansions. Shopping, of course, is mandatory and I had a field day buying lots of summery beach wear which I brought back for the girls in my family. My treat was to find a beautifully designed white linen outfit from a made-on-the-premises designer – an elegant creation which I have worn only once!

Well, I did have a job to come back to and I shall probably never return.

A boat trip around the coast line had us oohing and aahing at the blue of the water. We headed for the famous Blue Grotto but we were immediately put off by the hordes of tourists queuing to go into the grotto. Our boat driver took us away to another equally beautiful spot that was completely deserted. Here we were able to jump in to the water and explore the wonders of the grotto.

Back on land, the rest of our stay consisted of eating, shopping and lazing by a pool. The food was fantastic, and we sampled some of the finest seafood I have ever had. The seafood in the region of course is plentiful and wonderful. Crab, clams, sardines, octopus, eel, mackerel. You name it, it was there, all my favourite seafood. One of the memorable meals on Capri was a dinner of Bolitto Misto. Why was that so memorable? On our first visit to this particular Italian restaurant we had enjoyed fairly typical and delicious food. The overly attentive waiter asked if we had any preferences. I asked if they did Bolitto Misto – a classic of North Italian cuisine, tough but delicious cuts of mixed meat made tender by hours of gentle simmering in a herb broth. It wasn't on the menu but if we returned in two night's time, they would oblige. The meal was all the sweeter for it having been specially prepared for us.

That waiter was particularly funny in that on our first visit to the restaurant, he flirted outrageously with me. Such flowery words of flattery abounded. All taken with a grain of salt I might add. After all I wasn't exactly ignorant of the flirting prowess of Italian men. In fact, he was such a confidence trickster that he arranged for us to hire his brother in law for our trip next day to the Grotto. On top of that, when we returned for the Bollito Misto, at the table behind us, the exact same words were being gushed over another woman of a certain age. Obviously, great PR for the restaurant, women came back for more flattery no doubt.

Next stop Rome. A ferry across to Naples then another fantastic train hurtling along at 280 km an hour and so smooth, not a drop of wine spilled as we ate our lunch!

As I had only ever been in Rome in wintertime, I wasn't prepared for Rome in the summer. Hot, dusty, unbearably crowded and made even more unattractive by the overabundance of beggars, many of them gypsies from Eastern Europe. They were extremely aggressive in their begging. They didn't say much, certainly not in English. They simply thrust grubby hands into my face and when rebuffed they resorted to what I can only guess were obscenities in their native tongue.

Nevertheless, our hotel was all that could be desired, elegant, comfortable and very stylish. Expensive, too, but *what the hell*, this was to be our last stop.

I took the boys for Bellinis at the famous Harry's Bar where I'd had so much fun all those years ago. We did lots of walking, ate more fabulous food, sampled some very fine Chianti and generally dodged the beggars.

I actually took a ride on one of those tourist buses, I was all walked out. This was just fine as I sat atop the bus and had a grand view of the hustle and bustle of the city. The Vatican was vastly different from what I had once experienced. Then, I simply walked in to St. Peter's, wandered around, went down into the catacombs and up on to the roof, inside the vast dome. All of this was done unfettered and uninterrupted. Nowadays, security and crowds make such an adventure impossible. I realise how fortunate I had been back then to be able to just go my own way.

Time came to leave the 'Eternal City' and in spite of the heat, the crowds, the beggars and the inflated prices, like Paris, it still has enormous charm.

My travels with the Craigs was a joy. Craig Murchie is a Master Mariner and Craig Bennett is a journalist and television personality specialising in Hollywood gossip. They are both erudite and funny, possessed of humour and fun loving ways. Craig Bennett is the more flamboyant of the two and has a wicked way with words (he'd love that alliteration!). Murchie has great organising skills, probably due to his training and experience as a ship's captain. His is the voice of reason and stability. That's why we often call him 'Captain Sensible'.

They are such great companions and Craig Murchie's organising skills are unbeatable. I had not one 'tourist' worry the entire time. Along the way we shared great times, food, wine and laughter, the core of our friendship. It wasn't so much a *Travels with My Aunt* as *Travels with Teet and Pop* ... and that's a private joke that I don't expect you to get.

My next adventure with 'Teet' and 'Pop' was the much-anticipated trip to the USA. We took off at the end of September 2015, a little over two months before my appeal was to be heard in Victoria. Surprisingly there was no objection to my leaving the country. I wasn't too sure as to what sort of company I would be with such a cloud hanging over me. I had no doubt that the boys would lift my spirits.

We arrived in Los Angeles and then boarded the flight for New York. JFK airport was as frenetic as all international airports and after much delay, we found our car and headed in to NYC. Of course, the traffic was horrendous, it was night time and the streets were gridlocked as the United Nations was in session and the city was awash with presidents and other dignitaries from all over the world.

We were booked in to the Lotos Club on E66th street. This gracious old club had originally been established as a gentlemen's club. Its founders were primarily young writers, critics and poets. The name was taken from Alfred, Lord Tennyson's poem 'The Lotos-Eaters.' The club always had a literary and artistic bent and boasted a noted collection of American paintings and a vast library. The atmosphere was certainly one of elegance and old-world charm. It's list of members reads like the who's who of America, arts, politics and business. Names as diverse as Dwight D. Eisenhower, Stephen Sondheim, Elaine Stritch, Andrew Carnegie, Isaac Stern, Orson Welles, William Randolph Hearst ... the list goes on.

The next day a visit to Central Park – literally five doors away and across Park Avenue. Global warming was evident in the park, in as much as the autumn leaves had not begun to turn. It was, in fact, like high summer and I was so disappointed because I had the words of the old song ringing in my ears, 'Autumn in New York' and as it was early fall, I expected to see the magnificent russets, browns and gold of a northern autumn.

Nevertheless, it was a delight to stroll through that iconic park in spite of the heat. I made my way to Strawberry Fields and the John Lennon memorial and there in that almost sacred site was a lone guitarist positively murdering the song, 'Imagine.' What a philistine!

Then it was lunch at PJs and the obligatory chicken soup, Reuben sandwich and iced tea. This is a landmark eatery and being lunch time, it was packed with wealthy old women and their carers. It was such an Upper East Side vibe.

A visit to the Metropolitan Museum of Art left us breathless with excitement and awe at the amazing exhibits. Exhibitions such as the vast Egyptian section that literally takes you back to the days of the Pharaohs. Massive pillars that could have come from a Hollywood bible epic but were, in fact, the Temple of Dendur, magnificent jewellery, gold carvings, 26,000 objects from the Palaeolithic to the Roman period. Far too much to appreciate in one viewing, we would have needed days to have done it full justice. Time was our enemy and I know that one could still spend days in there and still not see all the treasures on display.

Then we were off to Lafayette and to a lunch at the Lobster Pot, fresh, delicious lobster on a crusty roll with a superb secret dressing. That night a trip to the theatre to see James Earl Jones and Cicely Tyson in *The Gin Game*, a classic play for two older actors. In this case, these titans of the American theatre were eighty-four and ninety-one respectively and showed just why they are the legends that they are. Unforgettable.

Our visit to the 9/11 memorial and museum is very difficult to describe. It's magnitude and emotional impact has a power beyond belief. Tears flowed as I made my way through the images of that horrendous attack.

On a lighter note, lunch followed at the famous Katz Deli, immortalised in the film, *When Harry met Sally*. There is even a sign dangling from the ceiling to point out the spot where the immortal lines, 'I'll have what she's having' were spoken. I guess if you felt like recreating that scene, there would possibly be someone to give you the Meg Ryan lines, or is that groans? I'm sure Meg and Billy Crystal didn't have to line up for an hour in the street, queue to get a table and then queue again to pay and get out. Heaven help you if you had lost the receipt! Departure was made very difficult by enormous security guards until you had provided proof of payment. The food was mediocre but the 'people watching' made up for it.

Dinner that night at The Friar's Club was a real treat. Once again ordinary food but wonderful atmosphere. The Friar's Club was like stepping back to the early days of the 20th century when it was founded in 1904. Great splendour in the stained-glass windows, the arches, the oak panelling. Great, carved, oak doors leading to the Barbra Streisand Room. We dined in the Frank Sinatra Room! The food was average fare, fish, roast, vegetables, plain desserts, but the atmosphere made up for it.

This private club is noted for its 'celebrity roasts' and boasts a membership of some of the funniest men and women from Richard Pryor, Jerry Seinfeld and Robin Williams to Lucille Ball, Carol Burnet, Phyliss Diller and Joan Rivers, Ed Sullivan and Bob Hope. The funniest entertainers ever to grace a stage, film or television have all been 'roasted' by their peers in this club.

A trip to the Guggenheim Museum on 5th Avenue didn't disappoint. The superb design by Frank Lloyd Wright and the amazing collection therein seemed to convey to me the essence of New York art and design.

Of course, a trip to New York is not complete without a visit to the Empire State Building and a Broadway musical. The building and the crowds didn't hold much joy for me. I think that building is firmly entrenched in my mind from movies like *An Affair to Remember* and *Sleepless in Seattle*. Those fantasies will do me more than the reality.

The musical that we chose was the extraordinary *An American in Paris*. Here we had not only the adaptation of a famous movie but the music of George Gershwin. The performers were everything I expected from the Great White Way, triple threats the lot of them – singing, dancing and acting up a storm. The male lead was not only a principal dancer with the New York City Ballet but he sang and acted like a dream. The female lead was a very Leslie Caron type and like the star of the 1951 film, she was elfin and beautiful with dazzling dance skills.

The whole experience was quintessentially New York. Broadway at its best and to top it off, we were in the famous Palace Theatre, which had been the scene of many a great performance from Judy Garland and Marlene Dietrich to our very own *Priscilla, Queen of the Desert* starring my much-loved friend, Tony Sheldon. If the walls of that theatre could talk …

Next was a short trip to Nantucket a brief break from the noise, crowds and heat of the city.

This picturesque island off Cape Cod has a rich history of whaling as is evident in the Whaling Museum which also features an amazing collection of Scrimshaw, the fabulous artwork created by whalers, the carving, engraving and scrollwork done in bone or ivory, specifically, whale bone.

Strict building codes ensure that the historic beauty of the island and its unpainted cedar-shingle houses remains unsullied. Some areas of its coastline have been eroded by the treacherous Atlantic Ocean, so much so that a number of houses have been moved back, away from the cliff edge to avoid the inevitable slide into the ocean.

Delicious seafood abounds, and we feasted on such delights as oysters, crays, Quahog chowder and lobster bisque. Our final night there we dined at the quaintly named 'Brotherhood of Thieves' restaurant. The name is taken from the title of a pamphlet written by Stephen S. Foster which had vigorously attacked those who continued to support slavery. Foster is known for such American folk classics as *Camptown Races* and *Beautiful Dreamer*.

After a couple of restful days, it was back to NYC to prepare for the flight to LA.

A ninety-minute ferry trip around the Hudson River provided a history of the bridges, tunnels and workings of the harbour.

A poignant story by the guide told of a Brooklyn fireman, who, having missed the call to the World Trade Centre on that fateful morning, donned his full pack and ran nearly 3 km through the tunnel to join his comrades at the site. Sadly, he didn't survive that horrendous day along with so many other first responders. To this day, fire fighters, with full pack, stage an annual race through that tunnel in his honour.

I found New York to be the vibrant, wonderful city that I had expected, all that is good and not so good seems to be there. It held no surprises for me as a lifetime of movie going had me familiar with everywhere I went.

So, back to LA, the last leg of the trip.

We stayed in a Spanish style, suburban house, via the Airbnb network.

It was pleasant enough and in West Hollywood, handy to everything and suited us well.

The heat in LA was enervating. Thank God for air conditioning in the car. Of course, driving was the only way to get around. Grateful for the company and local knowledge of the boys, I was more than happy to be driven around this sprawling city.

They took me up to the various canyons and pointed out homes of stars. My very own tour guides who pointed out everything from the public toilets where George Michael was arrested to the site of the house where Sharon Tate was murdered. I saw Rudolph Valentino's mansion, Zsa Zsa Gabor's estate where apparently at the age of ninety-eight she was often propped up in bed by her equally aged husband to give audience to her fans. And all the while, hilarious anecdotes and quips from Craig B. While we were there Craig B. did frequent broadcasts back to Australia with his gossip news and also interviewed a couple of TV notables.

We sampled as much local fare as we could and dined at places like Nat & Al's and Canters. We sampled Mexican cuisine, burgers and the obligatory fried chicken, candied yams and collard greens. Massive helpings being the norm. Heaven help the waistline!

We took a trip to the movie actors retirement village and collected dear Helen Reddy and off we went to Malibu for fish and chips and frozen yoghurt. We also had dinner with her at Herb Alpert's restaurant/night club, Vibrato and listened to some very classy jazz.

High on my list of memorable visits, is a trip to the Getty Museum. I was speechless with delight at this magnificent building atop a mountain. It houses an extraordinary collection of Impressionists, Constables, Modern American Art and a breathtaking display of bronzes, *The Victorious Youth* by Lysippus. An unforgettable finish to my trip.

As we made our way back to Australia, I reflected on the trip. The crowds, the heat, the traffic all paled into insignificance as I recalled the energy, beauty and vibrancy of that country. Not to forget the fun I had experiencing it in such wonderful company.

I don't know that I was the best travelling companion for the boys given what faced me back home, but I am eternally grateful for their company, patience and kindness.

CHAPTER FIFTEEN

THE TRUTH SHALL SET
YOU FREE (MAYBE)

When I wrote of my first encounter with the legal system, I had hoped that writing about it would prove to be therapeutic. That most certainly was *not* the case. As I write this I have strong memories of the anxiety I felt back then as December 7 and the appeal hearing grew closer.

On the first day of the hearing, I was happily saved from the media horde by a most fortuitous demonstration of Trade Unionists from the Construction, Forestry, Maritime, Mining and Energy Union, blocking the streets where I had to pass. I was able to slip unnoticed through the crowd to the chambers of my Barrister, Justin.

A lengthy briefing was held, and it was decided that I would take the stand and be questioned. Justin and Stephen then proceeded to question me most vigorously in order to prepare me for what might come. As the testimony of Geoffrey and Jo-Anne at the first appearance was so impressive, it was decided not to call again. In fact, their testimony and the recording of my interview was deemed sufficient enough not to over complicate matters by calling further witnesses.

Off we went to the County Courthouse, uninterrupted as the media pack were still occupied with the demonstration. Whatever the reason for such a huge gathering, I am still, to this day, most grateful for the diversion. God bless the CFMEU!

This time in court I had not only Caitlin with me but also my grandson

Daniel, his soon to be wife, Brittany, my dear friends Elspeth Ballantyne and Wendy Becher and a number of Caitlin's old school friends who were prepared to speak for me as they had known me since they were teenagers.

The hearing began, and my accuser was called first. As before, she had a closed court but this time, she was not secreted behind a screen.

Questioning began, and my barrister cross examined her most vigorously. After some time, she seemed to be a little agitated and called for a break. This was granted, and she left the courtroom to go to the bathroom accompanied by her legal team. My family and friends waiting in the foyer then witnessed a most peculiar scene whereby she loudly berated her legal team for 'not looking after her.'

I wasn't *quite* sure what she meant by that.

Justin's cross-examining continued as did his questioning of the psychiatrist who had treated her during her troubled teenage years. His information was very revealing and shed even more light on her mental state at the time of the alleged offence.

Eventually, I was called, and my questioning was extremely brief. I answered a simple 'No' to Justin's question as to whether I had committed the alleged offence. The prosecutor then asked me a couple of peculiar questions, like what sort of dog I had owned back then, what type of car I drove then and what was I cooking when the alleged offence took place.

We then adjourned until the next day when we would return for the judge's verdict.

Naturally a fairly sleepless night followed as I pondered my future if the verdict was unfavourable. A brief summing up next morning by the judge and then his verdict.

I was acquitted.

My relief and that of my family and friends was indescribable. Nonetheless I felt bruised and deeply affected by the whole dreadful experience.

Of course, this joyous result received *absolutely minimal coverage by the media* who months before had savaged me unmercifully on their front pages and lead stories. Now, I doubt whether the reporting of the result rated any more than a short column on, say, probably page six ... teen!

Ah, well, yesterday's news, today's fish and chip wrapping as the old saying goes.

In the midst of the euphoria over the verdict, I was approached by the prosecutor as I was leaving. She shook my hand and said that, in her opinion, the case should never have come to court. She was gracious and dignified in defeat and I must mention that amid the black of her robes, she wore a stunning pair of bright red high heeled shoes. A classy lady.

I found her reaction rather telling and once again it set me wondering about the motives that sometimes govern the actions of the DPP. Why was my case pursued? Was it the old 'tall poppy' situation, was I a 'celebrity' scalp to be won? I'll never know but sometimes I wonder about other cases involving people of some note.

Throughout the whole ordeal from August to December, I was swamped with waves of support. I don't have social media access, but I am assured that communications between interested parties was rampant. My family bore the brunt of some very unsavoury reactions. These were kept from me, but I have no doubt they would have been very disturbing. The very nature of the internet and social media brings out the worst in some people, especially cowards who can hide in the murky world of anonymous postings. Overshadowing the negative comments was a tsunami of support, from fans and from colleagues and friends, among them a woman whom I have never met, Rhiannon is her name and I believe she set up a web site of support for me. To people like her I am eternally indebted. Such kindness gives me faith in the decency of people.

Having been exonerated from the nightmare, it was time to get on with my life.

The scars of that ordeal remain.

And I sought help when it was needed. I had never thought myself to be so vulnerable, but then I guess for every action there is a reaction and mine was diagnosed as PTSD by my doctor. I allowed myself to give in to it and seek help with a counsellor and for some time it was of benefit to me but frequently I find myself slipping back into the gloom of that experience. I feel that I have become somewhat of a grump these days and my old joy of living seems to have forsaken me. Of course, life isn't all doom and gloom. My happiness still lies with my family and friends and is now all the richer by the addition to the family of my great granddaughter, Amelia.

I am often asked what effect this trauma in my life had on me.

The court case, in monetary terms cost me nearly $40,000. It's not easy to come up with $40,000 at short notice and not knowing if it's just going to be money down the drain. But having been *eventually* exonerated I was awarded costs and so recovered the expenses I had incurred.

The emotional recovery was not so great. Even with the 'help' of the PTSD diagnosis and the support of the psychologist it was not an easy ride. I was distressed for myself, but I was equally distressed for the effect that it had on my family.

None of us escaped the nightmare and the ignominy of it all.

To this day, flashbacks occur to moments of those two and a half years, the drive on the highway after the phone call from police, the vile portrayal of me by the media, running the gauntlet of media packs on the street, the vitriol of the magistrate and the initial guilty verdict.

The real injustice is that when you are accused of a crime of this nature, the principal of the 'presumption of innocence' goes out the window. You are, de facto, presumed guilty until proven innocent.

And you are *tainted*. Even when due legal process has run its course and you are found innocent there is a small stain that never *quite* washes off.

Try as I might to avoid it I can't help but make a small observation that requests for my work have dried up since that time in 2015.

Maybe I'm just being paranoid.

Maybe it's just a reluctance on the part of producers to hire and for directors to cast older actresses – a reality that any female performer above a certain vintage will attest to. Whatever it is I have felt decidedly sidelined since then.

Before embarking on this auto-biography business, I wondered just how much of the 'inner' me I was prepared to share.

Although I have always enjoyed reading about other people's lives, I have never regarded my life as particularly interesting. All the memoirs of politicians, show business folk or historical characters that I have read have given me great delight and knowledge.

For example, when reading of other people's relationships, I wonder sometimes what other directions mine might have taken.

The old 'if only' questions pop up time and again.

If only my marriage had succeeded. *If only* I hadn't been so unwise in my relationship choices.

I delight in the success of my friends' relationships. To see the couples I love still so happy together after twenty, thirty, forty and even fifty years together. Interestingly, the most successful surviving relationships are same-sex ones.

Having been solo for a long time, I sometimes ponder the growing old together story. Would I have managed it? Having realised long ago that I am hopeless at relationship choices, I often ask myself if I could, indeed, bear the intimate company of a partner for all those years.

Somehow, I think not.

Am I too selfish? Yes, I probably am. Not selfish with material things but perhaps a bit too self-centred and selfish with my 'me' time.

However, it is all irrelevant now. Having reached the age that I have, I revel in my solitude and also in the company of friends and family, always a source of great love and happiness for me.

When I began this book I wondered where it would take me.

It is one thing to have life's memories locked away in the privacy of one's own heart and mind. It's another thing to expose those memories to the outside world.

I hope I have been as frank as possible. Revisiting some of those memories has at times been painful. At other times the journey into the past has been somewhat joyful, if tinged at times with a little bitter-sweet melancholy.

As Dame Edna Everage might say, I am now in the 'afternoon teatime of my life.'

This, inevitably, brings me to the subject of aging.

I have read of so many people who have welcomed and embraced their twilight years. I read of super-active octogenarians, running, jumping and never standing still. They have embarked on new careers, new educations and all manner of uplifting activities.

I, for better or worse, seem to have missed out on whatever gene it is that embraces those energies.

I'll admit that I am not relishing this most inevitable aspect of life.

In many respects I think I have become the proverbial grumpy old woman. I find so many things that really annoy me about society today. The dumbing down that has occurred via the media, the sloppy use of the English language, the 'Me, Me, Me' narcissism and the iniquitous treatment of the vulnerable – the refugees, the Indigenous peoples of this land, the homeless and the old.

I am still a political and news junkie although too often the presenting of the latter leaves a lot to be desired.

I grieve for the planet and what we have done to it. My generation has a great deal to answer for. The shining hope that I see is in those young people who have put aside their electronic devices, walked out of the classroom and demanded action from their elders in the hope that something might be done to protect their futures.

Although I have had a long, and some might say successful career, I can only state again that I have only ever thought of myself as a jobbing actor. The highs have been wonderful and the lows spectacular.

People who aren't in the entertainment game have the impression that it's all premiers and catwalks, bulb flashes and glamorous parties with rich, beautiful, witty an oh-so-privileged lives.

But, and I don't want this to turn into a pity party, especially so late in this book, but an acting career, like the career of any performing artist – singer, musician, dancer, what have you – does come with its costs. You never really stop paying your dues. People hold you to a higher standard, but I can tell you from the inside, entertainers aren't better people than everybody else, they really are just like everybody else – well, maybe a bit more so. And they're not as privileged as you might think. Acting is a career in which you can thrive, but it's also something that, to some extent, you survive.

But, well – mustn't grumble.

In the main, acting has given me a full life with all the attending hiccups.

I have made wonderful friends, met inspiring people and seen more of the world and my country than I would have otherwise.

I doubt very much if a theatre role will come my way again. I wonder at the wisdom of attempting eight shows a week. I have no doubts about my mental ability but as my mobility seems to be somewhat compromised, I doubt I could go the distance. Well, maybe a sit-down role. A fight scene or a lively dance routine would probably see me in a coma!

How I envy my idols, Dench, Smith, and all those other wonderful character actresses in England who show no signs of retiring. Happily, the work seems to be always there for them and 'Good for them!' I say.

Sometimes I toy with a feeling that I think is a small sadness that comes with the sense that an integral part of one's life is over. In some societies, the elderly are valued for their life's experiences. Sadly, that doesn't seem to be the case in the youth-obsessed world of today.

As people who have reached a certain vintage are often asked, I too am often asked if I have any advice to pass on.

Do I have words of wisdom to share?

I doubt that I am 'fount-of-deep-matters' wise.

Like many I have made monumental blunders on this rocky road of life. I like to think that those blunders have been balanced by some wise decisions. Like the venerable Paul Eddington of *Yes Minister* fame said before he died, in a very candid interview, that he hoped that he had not done much harm.

His exact words were:

'A journalist once asked me what I would like my epitaph to be and I said I think I would like it to be, "He did very little harm." And that's not easy. Most people seem to me to do a great deal of harm. If I could be remembered as having done very little, that would suit me.'

I too have endeavoured to live a life that didn't inflict too much damage on those around me. In the main I have succeeded. I have tried to be a good friend, a responsible citizen and above all a good mother. Yes, I have fallen down on a number of occasions but hopefully some innate goodness and common sense has prevailed.

Some people are really good at making the most of what they have been given, others are not so good. Mistakes must be made, lessons must be learned. I guess it boils down to the fact that life is what you make it in spite of the hurdles, many which you put in your own way.

It really comes down to, I think, about making the best of what you have been given.

And while there is ever a cryptic crossword to be done, a good book to read, a wonderful piece of music to listen to, a friend to share good food and a bottle of wine, a dog to pat or a great grandchild to delight in, then life is bloody good.

I wouldn't be dead for quids!

It ain't over until the fat lady sings and this fat lady has a few songs in her yet, I think.

Even if she does sound like a bullfrog.

Only taller.

First published in 2019 by New Holland Publishers
This edition published in 2022 by New Holland Publishers
Sydney • Auckland

Level 1, 178 Fox Valley Road, Wahroonga, NSW 2076, Australia
5/39 Woodside Ave, Northcote, Auckland 0627, New Zealand

newhollandpublishers.com

A record of this book is held at the National Library of Australia.

ISBN 9781760794385

Group Managing Director: Fiona Schultz
Project Editor: Xavier Waterkeyn
Proofreader: Elise James
Production Director: Arlene Gippert
Designer: Andrew Davies

Front cover photo: © Fremantle
Front cover inset photo © The Gordon Frost Organisation
Back cover photo: © Paul Schnaars

10 9 8 7 6 5 4 3 2 1

Keep up with New Holland Publishers on Facebook
 facebook.com/NewHollandPublishers
 @newhollandpublishers

www.ingramcontent.com/pod-product-compliance
Lightning Source LLC
Chambersburg PA
CBHW021226090426
42740CB00006B/396